CONNECT

CONNECT

How to Find Clarity

and Expand Your Consciousness

with Pineal Gland Meditation

ILCHI LEE

BEST
LIFE
MEDIA

BEST
LIFE
MEDIA

459 N. Gilbert Rd, C-210
Gilbert, AZ 85234
www.BestLifeMedia.com
480-926-2480

First paperback edition: July 2019
Library of Congress Control Number: 2019940471
ISBN-13: 978-1-947502-14-7

Cover and interior design by Kiryl Lysenka

This is my simple religion. There is no need for temples; no need for complicated philosophy. Our own brain, our own heart is our temple; the philosophy is kindness.

— Dalai Lama

Contents

Take Back Your Brain

Where in your life are you standing right now, and with what mindset? When you've reached the end of a busy day, and you're tucking yourself in for the night, what do you feel in your heart? Do you feel confident that your life has a direction, and that you are the one driving your life in that direction?

If you're up against a particular challenge right now, do you have faith that you can overcome it and move on? Do you feel a sense of fulfillment—that you've got a firm grip on the steering wheel of your life and are living the values that are meaningful to you? And more than anything, do you feel that you're deeply connected with yourself and that you truly love yourself?

I've written this book to help you confidently answer "Yes" to these questions.

Over the last 40 years, I've met with numerous people around the world as I've given countless lectures and workshops. The people I met were invariably immersed in a plethora of anxieties great and small, looking for solutions. Seeing this, I thought hard about how I could help relieve their suffering, if only a little.

So, I've created and taught many methods for recovering physical health, relieving mental anxiety, and developing happiness by reconnecting with the true self. Over the years, thousands of people of all ages and from all walks of life have benefited from the programs I have created, and I feel immense joy whenever I hear the testimonies of people who have been able to achieve a sense of well-being through these methods. Yet, I have never been satisfied that what I have offered is enough, so I am always looking to upgrade and refine what I present to people.

Recently I took a long look back at what I've been doing for the last four decades and at the problems people have repeatedly presented to me, such as stress-related illnesses, depression, anxiety, and relationship issues. The more I reflected upon these common worries, the more the underlying cause became clear to me: *people's connection with themselves has been cut.*

It's easy, and normal, to think that the causes of our problems are to be found outside ourselves, in other people or in the environment, but that's definitely not it. Dig deeper, and you'll ultimately find that the primary cause of your problems lies not in your relationship with other people or in some imperfection in the environment, but rather in your connection with yourself. Yes, the earth suffers from pollution, and the behaviors and words of others can be toxic, but the first order of business is your own inner world, not the world outside of you. In fact, you will never be able to adequately solve outside problems if the interior connection isn't established first. You experience physical ailments, from headaches and indigestion to much more serious diseases, because your connection with your body isn't good. And if you're troubled, unable to find direction in some area of life, you're not really connected with your true self.

We can see the problems that arise from disconnection in every aspect of our lives, from our individual selves to the ecosystems of the earth. There are more than two billion Facebook users worldwide with approximately 300 friends per user, but loneliness has surfaced as a greater public health risk than smoking. People may have a lot of social media friends, but they don't have that many true friends to turn to in real life, to talk to and share their hearts with comfortably.

The greatest challenges faced by humankind today—such as climate change, gender inequality, the wealth gap, military conflicts, trade disputes, and religious conflicts—have at their roots a deep-seated mindset that separates me from you and humans from nature. A solution that's based on separation without consideration of mutual interests can never be a true or sustainable solution, and in the end such a "solution" disadvantages everyone. Unless we heal the disconnection that is so widespread in our lives, the hole in our souls will keep getting bigger, the conflict between different social groups will grow increasingly serious, and the Earth's environment will reach a state in which recovery is impossible.

Once you understand that disconnection is the underlying cause of your problems, then the solution also becomes clearer. All you have to do is mend your broken connections. Recover your connection with your body, your connection with your true self, and your connection with people and the world.

How can we recover that connection? I believe that the master key that makes it possible is in the human brain, and I present Pineal Gland Meditation as an essential technique for awakening the brain.

Thoughts, memories, and intellectual knowledge are what most people typically associate with the brain. However, the brain doesn't only contain the artificial information that we've accumulated during our lives. There is a certain something in our brain that is original and fundamental. Before we had thoughts, emotions, experiences, or knowledge, there existed complete and pure energy and consciousness. We could also call this nature, the rhythm of life, or even the divinity within us.

What brings separate individuals together is the universal homogeneity that exists in people beyond their personal differences. I feel that we can find that homogeneity in the pure consciousness and energy inside us. I believe it's that pure consciousness that ties together not only human beings, but all life forms and ultimately everything that exists.

I have dedicated my life to exploring the brain and developing and sharing methods to use it well, because that kind of pure consciousness and energy exists within our brains. I believe that by recovering this consciousness, we can know ourselves as we truly are and recover our connection to all things in existence. I am certain that when we recover such a connection, we can gain the true solution and insight to simultaneously solve individual problems and the Earth's problems. It is with these aims that I blended the ancient Korean mind-body training methods of the Sundo tradition with neuroscience to establish Brain Education, and why I have taught brain meditation for decades.

The human brain is the master key that can overcome separation and connect all things. And within the brain, the organ that acts as the channel to pure consciousness and energy is the pineal gland, located in the central part of the brain. The Pineal Gland Meditation introduced in this book presents the principles and process for recovering this pure consciousness by revitalizing the function of the pineal gland.

To fully utilize the power of the brain and the pineal gland, I suggest taking a different perspective on the brain. Rather than seeing the brain only as an anatomical organ, I see it as the embodiment of human character. You could say that your brain is the holistic expression of your physical, mental, and spiritual essence. Therefore, being connected with your brain means meeting with your essential nature.

When you understand that your brain is the embodiment of

your essence, you can converse and interact with it. That's when you can use your brain to change your life and transform the world. I hope that through this book you will be able to resonate deeply with this aspect of the brain, and that through Pineal Gland Meditation you will experience a sincere and powerful encounter with your brain.

The moment you're connected with your brain, you will meet with the limitless energy and life within you. You will have a spine-tingling feeling for how powerful, beautiful, and divinely sacred your essential nature is. That electric excitement and pure poignance will spread throughout your brain and your heart and your whole body, bringing fundamental change to your life and world.

The Pineal Gland Meditation that I introduce in this book could be called the "pinnacle of Sundo meditation," a way of developing body, mind, and soul to completion that grew out of the ancient practice of Sundo. Once your insight has been awakened through Pineal Gland Meditation, you'll realize that seemingly separate, isolated things are actually all connected. You'll perceive things you couldn't see before, and by looking at yourself, others, and the world with a broader perspective, your empathy, understanding, and tolerance will grow. With eyes that see connection and unity, you'll find solutions to problems caused by looking at the world as a place of separation and isolation.

Experiencing this new consciousness, opening these new eyes, is truly a fundamental solution to our problems. When you awaken to that one great thing, you'll also develop the power to find solutions to other, more trivial problems.

But what role does the pineal gland play in this awakening process? Physically speaking, it is a tiny and seemingly insignificant organ—a type of endocrine gland located deep within the brain. It is known to regulate the biological clock of the human body, including circadian rhythms and reproductive cycles. In many spiritual practices, it is associated with the sixth chakra, or "third eye," the center of intuition and spiritual perception. In Pineal Gland Meditation, it is understood as the center of spiritual connection in the brain. It could be thought of as a plug that can be connected to an outlet. Everyone has this "plug" deep within their brain, but it is up to each of us to connect it to the "outlet," the source of divine, cosmic energy.

For most people in modern society, this connection has been lost, but Pineal Gland Meditation offers a way to recover this natural ability. In the moment that you "plug in" through Pineal Gland Meditation, you will develop the power to understand yourself truly and to embrace others with tolerance. While you meditate with your eyes closed, the waves of peaceful but powerful changes arising within you will spread to the whole of your life. And the world you see after opening your eyes will have changed, now appearing utterly different from what it was before.

All of us have the power to create the life that we want and change the world into a better place. But in order to use that power, your consciousness must be awake. Otherwise you lose your self-efficacy, and it's easy to let yourself be pulled around by your habits, external information, or the societal environment or systems.

When you focus on your inner world to feel and connect with your self, you can find your absolute value beyond comparisons and judgment. People who have found that value are able to live their authentic lives, not the lives dictated or expected by society or other people. To do this, you need to "take back your brain." You must take it back from thoughts and habits that no longer serve you, the false limitations inside and outside of you that whisper in your ear, "Nope, not you. You can't do it." Or, "The world has always been like that. Nothing's going to change."

In the past, people who had lots of intellectual knowledge were considered smart. Nowadays, doing a search on the internet gives anyone relatively easy access to pretty much all knowledge. More knowledge is not the solution now. In this present era we need the penetrating insight to see to the heart of problems, the innovation and creativity to find answers outside the box, the executive faculty to move from knowing to action, and the wisdom to connect and integrate what was separated. But, this does not come through intellectual knowledge. Instead, it happens when you connect and interact with the world in a way that goes beyond the patterns of your habitual thoughts and behavior, creating a world that transcends our current human-made systems. Pineal Gland Meditation will connect you to that world.

This book will guide you on a four-part journey to connect with yourself.

In Part I, we look at the problems that arise in all areas of life due to disconnection from yourself, and we explore the map of complete connection with your true self, as presented through the Korean Sundo tradition.

Part II leads you through training that connects your body, soul, and divinity based on the principles and methods of energy development taught in Sundo. You will be guided step by step through Pineal Gland Meditation.

In Part III, I'll introduce you to the five steps of Brain Education, which will connect you with your brain to become the true master of your life. I'll also teach two innovative and powerful methods of meditation that awaken the pineal gland. I've included a number of new and important ideas in this section, so please be sure to read it.

Part IV presents testimonials from individuals who have transformed their lives through Pineal Gland Meditation, along with my own pineal gland story. Through these stories, you'll be able to gain inspiration about what kind of transformation you can bring to your life and to the world through Pineal Gland Meditation.

In the epilogue to this book, I share my vision and what I imagine and hope in terms of the new possibilities and new world that we can create together when many people recover their sense of connection and oneness.

You will see certain key ideas repeatedly discussed throughout the book. Please know that I did this intentionally to help you fully grasp them and to help the important points stick in your mind.

Traditionally, Pineal Gland Meditation has been known as a very advanced level of meditation. That's why there are many people who think that it can only be practiced by well-seasoned masters of meditation who have engaged in spiritual practice for a long time. However, this is a misconception. The essential goal of Pineal Gland Meditation is to empty yourself of the thoughts, emotions, and information that cause disconnection from who you really are, and then recharge and fill that space with the infinite energy of life and bright consciousness. Anyone with a normal brain can practice Pineal Gland Meditation and experience that power. Many people are already recovering the health of their bodies and minds through Pineal Gland Meditation at the hundreds of Body & Brain Yoga centers and meditation centers around the world, and they are experiencing the shift to a positive lifestyle.

I believe that everyone can plug into the infinite field of cosmic energy and pure consciousness, just as I did long ago. Everyone holds the potential to awaken, especially when given tools such as Pineal Gland Meditation. That absolute faith has been a lamp guiding me for several decades, its bright light enabling me to view others and the world with hope, even in moments of distress and frustration.

I believe in you and trust that you will find your way to reconnect with true self, the fundamental solution to your most pressing problems, and that you can confidently live as a master of your brain and your life. And I cheer you on with all my heart. I've put my faith in you—my earnest desire for you to succeed—into each and every sentence of this book. I hope my mind will touch your mind, the reverberations in my heart reaching your heart with living vitality.

When you read this book, imagine that you're talking directly with me. I want at times to be a friend, fully understanding your pain and suffering; at times to be your counselor, getting right to the point you were not aware of; and at times to serve as your trainer, sitting before you and teaching you energy-training methods and meditation, step by step.

Spring 2019
Ilchi Lee

PART I

Connecting with Yourself

CHAPTER 1

Why Are So Many People Today Afraid and Frustrated?

Our modern technological age has solved many of the problems that our ancestors faced. In the developed world, most people have enough to eat, access to education, and a warm place to sleep at night. Theoretically, we should be happy and carefree, going about our lives without any significant worries.

Yet, that is not the case. Diseases caused by stress are on the rise, and more and more people are suffering from long-term mental problems like clinical depression, anxiety attacks, and bipolar disorder. Incidents of violence are becoming commonplace news, and incivility online and on the road is now part of everyday life. Clearly, technology alone cannot solve our problems, so what, if anything, can we do?

First, we can understand that problems are simply inevitable. In the course of life, everyone faces many difficulties. In fact, it's no exaggeration to say that our lives consist of a series of troubles, since there are always obstacles to overcome. Some problems are easy to solve, while others are too much to bear, causing us prolonged hardship and suffering. One might say that life is a training field, where over time we cultivate the ability to handle and solve life's problems with greater ease and grace as they rush over us one after another. Since problems are an inevitable part of life, it's important to take ownership of your problems and to develop a habit of diagnosing and resolving them yourself.

People who regularly practice managing their own issues know how to take charge of their lives. They handle things well, from the small stuff like dressing, washing, eating, cleaning, and sleeping, to the more important things like developing positive relationships, doing well in school, and taking care of their own health and wellbeing. Such people have true confidence, exhibiting the power to deal well with whatever big problems come their way.

Those who lack such practice, though, failing to manage problems in their lives, are easily jerked around by them. Moreover, if their experience of failing to solve problems continues to build up, they will lose confidence and self-esteem. In fact, our problem-solving ability determines our success in life. If we are born into a bad environment, or if we face difficulties later in life, it is the only thing that will help lift ourselves up. If we make a bad choice or develop a bad habit, it is the only thing that can help us turn around. Thus, developing our problem-solving ability is a shortcut to improving our quality of life.

A good first step toward developing good problem-solving ability is to determine how and when problems arise. How do problems develop and what kinds of problems are we likely to experience? Although there are countless problems that people face in life, most of them relate to these five aspects of life: health, sex, money, reputation, and death.

When you consider these five categories, which feels most serious to you in your life at this moment? If you're physically ill, then health will be your greatest concern. If you're in a love relationship, then perhaps you'll worry most about problems with your partner. If under financial pressure, you'll be most focused on your money problems. If you're sensitive to social status or the opinions of the people around you, you'll fret over your reputation. If you're suffering from a severe illness or in your old age, feeling you don't have much time left, you'll worry about death. So, whatever is most pressing to you at the moment will feel like the most important kind of problem to you.

How serious problems feel subjectively differs depending on the circumstances an individual faces. An issue that is trivial to some people might be of intense concern for others. Feeling that a problem is serious simply means that you're hung up on it; you don't know what to do about it, and it is threatening to change your life in some negative way. In other words, the problem has you trapped, and you won't feel free until it is solved. In Buddhism, this is viewed as part of a person's karma, which dictates that every individual is born with particular questions they must study in this life.

So, what's your biggest concern right now? What troubles you and causes you to worry? What is it that makes you frustrated and uncomfortable? I suggest that you view whatever makes you most concerned and uneasy as part of the basic question you'll have to solve on your journey through life. If you are like most people, you have troubles for which you have not yet found solutions, although you want to find them. Why not pause right now and write down, one by one, any problems that come to mind? You could make a separate list for each category: health, sex, money, reputation, and death.

Many of the problems we face involve personal relationships. On practically a daily basis, we see difficulties arise in our relationships with our loved ones, close friends, coworkers, and even strangers. These types of problems affect us emotionally, often more deeply than other types of problems. In particular, troubles with people whom we trust to love and support us can shake the very roots of who we are, right to the foundation of our being. If this has happened to you, it will be an important and difficult obstacle to overcome.

Our working lives also tend to be a source of trouble, bringing up issues involving money and reputation. The drive to be successful in our career and the burden of responsibility it brings creates a lot of stress in our lives. For many of us, it undermines our self-confidence and sense of self-worth, especially when we compare ourselves to others who have succeeded beyond us. "If I'd only been a little smarter, a little more capable . . ." we tell ourselves.

Outer appearance is also a nagging concern for many people, a source of reputation problems. Usually, men long to have robust, muscular bodies, and women to have slim, sexy figures, with beautiful faces and skin. And, whenever we go out, wearing up-to-date fashion and keeping an attractive hairstyle is a small but constant worry.

Correcting bad habits is another big problem to solve, one that greatly affects our health and reputation. Some people are unable to escape addiction to alcohol, tobacco, games, overeating, or drugs. They resolve many times to correct these habits, challenging themselves to do so, but then feel frustration and shame when they see themselves returning to their old habits. Idleness and laziness, negative ways of thinking and talking, criticizing and blaming others—these are also negative habits that need to be solved and that require great self-awareness and honest internal inquiry to solve.

While we may have specific problems we can point out and talk about in this way, there's another kind of problem that doesn't show on the surface but may be pulling us down. It's quite common, but most people can't even recognize that it's happening; they assume that it's just a normal part of life. It is the sense of emptiness and lethargy people feel when life has become stagnant, with no growth or change. Have you ever felt stuck? Have you felt like you're simply walking in place, trapped by inertia and repeating the same routine without any change or novelty? Has the passion in your heart long gone cold, and do you feel increasingly helpless and anxious that your life may never amount to more than this? If you say yes to any of these questions, you have experienced this problem.

Many people live repetitive lives without change or growth, today always the same as yesterday. They no longer dream. And they no longer challenge themselves to do anything beyond their comfort zone. Lethargy, depression, anxiety, isolation, frustration, a sense of inferiority, and a negative attitude slowly eat away at their brains. The real issue here is that they have failed to identify the cause of their problems accurately. Usually, instead of looking carefully within, they simply blame their situation and the people around them, negating their own power to find a solution. They neither try to see it clearly nor attempt to find the will to improve. At some point, they find themselves becoming spectators to their own lives. No one ever starts out stuck in a rut, but sometimes negative experiences turn into a pattern of learned helplessness.

When hopelessness and negativity become the norm, people are no different from the flea in the following story:

A flea was caught in a glass jar covered with a transparent lid. The flea jumped as hard and high as he could, but he hit the cover every time and was hurled to the bottom of the jar by the impact. Over time, the flea learned how to jump without getting hurt. He would jump only to a safe height, not touching the lid, before dropping again. Later, after the lid was removed, the flea continued to jump only to that same safe height. He kept jumping only as high as he could to keep from crashing into the lid, mistakenly believing that it was still there. We may be like this flea. To keep from getting hurt, do you also keep jumping only to the same height as before, sticking to the same predictable routine?

The reason we worry about various problems in life is actually rooted in a very positive human characteristic—the natural desire to be better than we are now. Or, to put it more simply, we want to be happier. So, in our pursuit of happiness, we strive day and night and pour our hearts into the people we love. As time passes, though, we learn that the world isn't the fairytale we thought it would be, and people aren't always as genuine as we'd hoped. We drink the bitter cup of failure as the results of our projects fail to meet our expectations. Though we work hard, we never get anywhere.

When this experience is repeated, negative thoughts automatically play in our heads: "There's no point in trying. I guess I'm unlucky." We end up choosing to be content with things as they are. "It's lucky I didn't fall behind. I'll just maintain the status quo instead of taking on a challenge that's too big for me and failing again." When failures pile up, we no longer want to take on new challenges. A circuit of negative thinking forms in our brains, so that attempting something new invariably causes negative thoughts to pop into our heads.

Such experiences affect our everyday habits, not only our work. Stuck in repetitive daily lives, we occasionally resolve to shake things up by attempting something new. At the start of every new year, we think about how to better ourselves, resolving to do everything from exercising and dieting (usually at the top of the list) to quitting smoking and drinking, getting up early, reading books, practicing self-development, and doing good works. But such resolutions typically peter out after a few days—something everyone experiences. When this is repeated, at some point we no longer make new plans or take on new challenges. We think, "Nothing I've done so far has worked out. Would that change now? How many days would my resolution last? It might last a few days, but that would be the end of it, once again." Negative brain circuits activate automatically in this way. We reach a point where we no longer trust ourselves, a point where even our credibility with ourselves hits rock bottom.

One significant time when the negative neural circuits of self-judgment are strengthened is when we're hurt in a personal relationship. The wounds are deeper, more painful, if we feel we have treated the other person sincerely, with an open heart. Look carefully into the human heart, and you'll find that almost no one is free of scars, large and small. What about your heart? Do scars from past wounds remain? Who gave you those wounds? Words spoken by our beloved parents, unintentionally or in anger, can haunt us, leaving open wounds. For example, let's say that a parent yelled at her young child, "You idiot. Why are you so stupid?" The impact of those words ripples through the vulnerable child's brain, even if they weren't spoken seriously. From then on, that message will repeat in the child's brain: "I'm stupid." The experiences of childhood greatly influence character formation, with some wounds failing to heal even in adulthood.

The wounds we receive when breaking up with a romantic partner are no small matter, either. We're hit hard when we realize that the love we once believed would never change was actually temporary, like rotting food past its expiration date. We close our hearts, trying not to show our scars, the wounds left by feelings of disappointment and betrayal. New love may come our way after time passes and we feel our wounds have healed to some extent. But what if that love, too, follows a similar pattern? When our text messages get no response and our phone calls go unanswered, when we learn that our partner wants to break up, we feel as if our very being has been rejected. Nothing stings quite so much as that. When such experiences are repeated, we close down our hearts. Why? Because we're afraid we'll be hurt again, afraid we'll be rejected again. From then on, we always maintain a certain distance in our relationships. We keep enough distance to not be hurt anymore—like the flea in the glass jar, not jumping above a certain height.

Why do we feel frustrated? We feel frustrated when we fail. We feel frustrated when we're rejected. We feel frustrated when we're unloved. We feel frustrated when we're hurt.

Why do we feel fear? We're afraid of making mistakes. We're afraid of failure. We're afraid of rejection. We're fearful of being unloved. We're fearful of being criticized. We're frightened that we will be hurt.

Because of such frustration and fear, many people no longer take on challenges, no longer open their heart, no longer get too close to others. They create their own boundaries—"I'll go this far and no farther." Whenever we do this, we live trapped inside the domain we've created, not realizing that it's a prison of our own making. Living that way, we think that we have been rejected by others. Think carefully about it, though. Could it be that we have actually alienated ourselves and rejected others, making ourselves unapproachable? It is us and no one else who have created those unseen boundaries, keeping others from invading our domain.

Why do any of us do that? Because we feel safe within our walls. Because we think it's dangerous to take even one step outside the safe zone we've created. But are we really safe there? Are we really happy and free? Isn't that unseen prison gradually blunting our edge, our sense of being? In our deep, inner consciousness, could we be disparaging ourselves, telling ourselves that we're not good enough or smart enough? That may be leading us to a place where, if our longing for change rears its head even a little, it gets smacked down, beaten back, and continuously numbed by the thought, "What am I supposed to do? I'll just live like this."

If this continues, our sense of being in the world—acting as a member of the human race connected with others in the world—grows feeble. An idea gradually encroaches on our brain, the thought that we can't actively direct our life. If this becomes extreme, we may even feel that ours is a useless existence, that it doesn't matter whether we live or die.

The biggest problem is that we're growing increasingly distant from ourselves. We don't think about how we can love ourselves better; instead, we judge ourselves, telling ourselves that we are not measuring up. We take on the role of our own worst critic, instead of our own best friend. In this feeling's more severe form, we abuse and even hate ourselves. On the outside, we seem to be getting along without much problem, but in our internal world, we keep punishing ourselves: "You're an idiot! You can't do anything right." We see in news reports what may happen if the situation deteriorates and an individual's inner critic grows out of control. Exploding in rage against other people and the world, that person becomes violent or quietly destroys themselves, alone.

People put in a lot of effort to fit in and gain status in other people's eyes. What we should really fear is becoming alienated from ourselves, not being alienated by others. The problem isn't others hating us, but our not loving ourselves. We are pushing ourselves away, not others doing so. It's a break in our connection with ourselves. This self-alienation, or loss of self, may very well be the most serious spiritual crisis we experience in these times.

I propose Pineal Gland Meditation, which is based on the mind-body training methods of ancient Korea, as one solution for these problems. But what is the pineal gland and why should it matter so much? The pineal gland is a pinecone-shaped endocrine gland in the brain. Anatomically, it's located slightly below and to the rear of the center of the brain, immediately behind the upper brain stem, which handles major vital functions such as breathing, pulse, and blood pressure. In diverse spiritual traditions, the pineal gland has symbolized the wisdom to see through the illusions of the world, elevated spirit, and ultimate knowledge, and is also known as the "third eye." Through this eye, we will discover a whole new way of seeing and solving our problems, approaching them from their very root.

Before learning the specific method of Pineal Gland Meditation, though, we must fully understand the reasons we need this form of meditation in our lives. That's why I devoted the first part of this book to describing those reasons as carefully and in as much detail as possible. Based on such an understanding, I want you to have hope and feel certain about it, telling yourself, "I really need this! My life could really change through this!" Sincerity is key to the success of this method, so please check yourself first. Vague curiosity is not enough, but if you're really ready to grow, please read on.

CHAPTER 2

Are You Connected with Yourself?

If you suggest to someone that she is disconnected from herself, she may not immediately acknowledge it, saying, "Not me. I'm connected with myself." But there are signs that appear when you've been disconnected from yourself. Check whether any of the following are happening in your own body and mind.

Do you find it hard to change negative emotional states or thought patterns? Did your hope or expectation of a better life vanish long ago? Do feelings of irritation or anxiety keep arising for no particular reason? Does your physical and mental energy feel depleted, or do you feel lethargy and lack of ambition in just about every area of life? Do you have a growing feeling of inner emptiness and a lack of direction or meaning in your life? Do you find yourself drowning in momentary pleasures to relieve your stress, like overeating, alcohol, gambling, drugs, or sex? Do you feel emotionally numb, tending to lose interest in the people or happenings around you? Are you cynical about yourself, disparaging, and unable to feel your own worth?

Everyone experiences highs and lows in life, so it is not un-expected to experience such things a few times in our lives. The problem is when negativity goes beyond a temporary experi-ence, becoming repetitive or routine. When this is the case, we are unmistakably becoming disconnected from ourselves—a condition without love for ourselves, of neglecting or hating ourselves, where inner wholeness and joy have disappeared.

I have discovered a single, powerful question that lets you diagnose whether you are disconnected from yourself: "Who am I?" Before asking yourself this question, close your eyes and concentrate carefully on the feelings in your heart. Then ask yourself with complete honesty and sincerity, "Who am I?" Listen for the answer that comes from within you. Try to feel the response that comes from your heart.

What answer do you hear? Who *are* you? Is your name who you are? Are your external appearance, your thoughts, your feelings, your experiences, and your knowledge who you are? Are your family or position in society, your profession, and your possessions who you are? These things are what you have, not who you are. Do you feel your true self—who you really are— existing without your nametag, without the knowledge or ideas you've accumulated? Does your being itself feel precious and beautiful, here and now, regardless of what you've achieved or failed to achieve?

Most people are confused, unable to find a satisfactory answer, when asked, "Who are you?" Even many philosophers and thinkers, grizzled veterans of life's adventure, and elders exploring the profundities of the spiritual struggle to respond with confidence to this question. In fact, it could be said that this one question—"Who am I?"—is the underlying concern of all spiritual traditions and philosophies, one that continuously eludes a final satisfactory answer.

You may have thought long and hard about this question at least once. But no matter how hard you've mulled it over, no matter how much you've asked those around you, no matter how many books you've rummaged through, you've probably been unable to find a satisfactory answer. "These questions are for people with too much time on their hands," some say. "I have no problem making a living and getting on with my life, even if I don't know who I really am." You may even have given up on finding an answer, seeing others apparently getting along just fine without seriously worrying about such things. Most often, we simply accept whom society tells us we are, defined by the roles we fill, and move on from there.

For many, the situation is truly ironic. Most people assume that they are responsible for their own lives, but are they really? They take great pride in achieving success and status in the world, but in reality they are just living according to commonly accepted ideas crammed into their heads by society, and society is rewarding them for that obedience. In the end, though, they are unable to escape a nagging sense of emptiness and dissatisfaction. It is undeniable that countless people live day in and day out without knowing who they truly are.

Is it really a big deal if you don't know who you are? Yes, it definitely is! Why? If you don't know who you really are, then who is the self, the "you," who's been living up to this point? You've been living as who, as what? After hearing such a question, you may feel stunned, as if you've been hit in the back of the head. To get to the truth of your situation, you have to ask yourself some hard questions: Whose life am I leading? Are these my thoughts, my emotions, and my desires?

When we say that someone is disconnected from themselves, we're referring to that person's true self. So, if you think, "Not me. I'm connected with myself," then you first need to take a look at who or what that self is. Carefully look within to see whether that self is just your thoughts, emotions, desires, and ideas, or whether it is your true self, living and breathing in your heart as your true essense, independent of outer conditions. Look at what you're currently connected with, what you're living for.

We need to discover who we really are *to escape from suffering*. If you dig deep, really deep, into the cause of all the suffering you feel in life, you'll realize that all your problems start there—in not knowing who your true self is, in not being connected with your true self.

What kinds of suffering and what problems develop when you're disconnected from your true self?

First of all, you don't know what your true self genuinely wants. Since you're unable to commune with it, even if the true self in your heart says, "This is what I want," you can't hear those words—or if you do hear them, you ignore them. That's because you've developed the habit of focusing on what your false self wants—your desires, emotions, and thoughts—rather than on what your true self wants.

Your false self, the egoic self, may be satisfied if you continue to lead such a life, but your true self can never be satisfied with this. Instead, you will feel empty and frustrated, asking yourself, "Is this really living well?" A never-ending desire for something better suggests that you haven't satisfied the true self inside, that you've been mainly using your energy to satisfy the wishes of your false self. It's as if, in the hot and humid days of summer when we should be watering the drooping flowers in the garden, we've been pouring the water out onto the street. It's understandable that people are wasteful and unproductive in life when they don't know what they should be focusing on.

Secondly, it's hard to find precise solutions to the issues you face if you are disconnected from your true self. In order to solve problems and make decisive choices, you first need to know what you really want. But to know that, you need to know what your *true self* wants. Normally, instead of being able to find this out, you may think hard about a particular problem, losing sleep, but rather than the real answer, reach a conclusion that momentarily satisfies your thoughts, emotions, or desires. You may flip back and forth among them, going with the energy acting most powerfully at a given moment. That's why your life seems to lack consistency, feeling unpleasantly chaotic.

Why such confusion and wandering? The root cause is not having a definite center inside. Put another way, you're not sure what your true self wants because you're disconnected from it. If you were connected with your true self, you would no longer have any reason to be confused.

The third problem that develops when you're not connected with your true self is that you're not sure what direction you should take in the future. What you really want isn't clear, so you can't find an exact goal or direction in life. You may end up being busy following others, living the way they live, just going with whatever works without knowing what you should look for or what kind of life you really want, and without a definite center all your own. It's easy to find yourself rushing this way and that, bewildered, until in the end, your life has become a series of regrets, haunted by the question, "What have I been living for?"

Ultimately, disconnection from your true self will negatively impact all areas of your life. First, when you're disconnected from yourself, you're disconnected from your body. You don't have good communication with your body, making it difficult to determine what it really wants, which is health. "Please make me healthy," our bodies say. But it's easy to follow the voices of our desires and emotions, failing to hear the true voices of our bodies. That's why, when under stress, so many people overeat or stuff them with sweets. They think that the body craves such food, but it's actually what the emotions want, not the body. "Please quit stuffing me with food," the body screams. "I'm full.

Quit cramming me with junk food and sweets. They're bad for me." This is true any time people lack self-control, such as when they spend too much time on the internet or procrastinate on important projects. Caught by stressful emotions, their brain ignores or no longer hears their body's voice.

"I'm feeling stiff and sore right now," our body may also say. "Don't just sit there, get me some exercise." But these demands are also often ignored by us. Irritable and lazy, the brain gets used to not moving all day, letting us sit there snacking and gripping the TV remote control whenever there is any free time. The brain is completely lost in TV shows, with sweet and greasy foods close at hand, so there's no way it will hear the body's voice. Occasionally relieving stress this way is okay, but making it a daily habit leads straight to obesity and disease. With the mind held by things outside the body, the body's sense for health and balance is gradually numbed. The more we lose self-awareness, the more we disconnect from our body and the true self inside.

Once you understand this, you'll see that even problems in your relationships are often due to issues with yourself, not problems with other people. Many people ask me how to resolve a problem they have with someone. "Try to focus first on yourself rather than worrying about your relationship with others," I advise them. "And love yourself more. Your relationships with others will get better when you truly understand yourself."

If you look closely and honestly, you'll see that your relationships with others reflect your relationship with yourself. You can love others only as much as you love yourself, and you can understand and tolerate others only to the extent that you understand and tolerate yourself. If you hate yourself, you will hate other people, too. How can you sincerely love others when you can't love yourself? If you take a good look at what's really going on, you'll see that even when people talk about sharing unconditional love, often they expect something from the other person—affection from others to fill the emptiness inside themselves. In fact, your level of attachment to others can be measured by the longing you feel: the needier you feel, the greater your attachment to the attentions of others.

Can you say that you truly know others if you don't know your true self first? And how can you make judgments, negative or positive, about the love of other people? If your connection with yourself isn't good, how can your connections with others be free of problems? If you can't accept yourself completely, how can you tolerate others, embracing them for who they are? The fundamental problem is your relationship with yourself. It's a question of how closely connected you are with yourself.

If resentment remains inside you—if you resent someone even a little—you're still not completely accepting and loving yourself. When you're able to love yourself, with your own shortcomings, you will be able to understand and tolerate the shortcomings of others, too. Restoring your relationship with yourself determines how much your relationships with others can improve.

However, people have a tendency to focus solely on their relationships with others, neglecting their connection with themselves. Sooner or later, fundamental problems emerge. You can be led about by other people, doing as they want to make them happy and receive their praise. But, when you don't get the hoped-for reaction, you will blame everything on the other person. If you are well connected with yourself, however, you can achieve balance in your relationships because you have a solid center—even if the other person hurts your feelings. More important than any relationship we have with someone else is the relationship we have with ourselves.

Being disconnected from yourself impacts the work you're doing, too. When you have no passion for your work, it loses its novelty, and you find yourself repeating the exact same pattern every day, today always the same as yesterday. Forcing yourself to smile like a soulless robot, you just keep doing what you've always done. People in this situation commonly think that the problem is the work itself, so they look for new work, work they can be passionate about. It would be great if they got lucky and found work in which they could excitedly immerse themselves. But many people, once their newfound work becomes familiar, again end up going through the motions, the same as before. If you keep repeating this pattern, then your work itself isn't the problem. You are the problem.

Passion is something you pull from within yourself, not something someone brings you from the outside. Work feels hard because your connection with yourself is tenuous; it doesn't engage you on a deep enough level to bring out your passion. How can joy and passion infuse in your work when you are disconnected from yourself, the most important thing? How can you be excited without knowing what it is that your heart really wants? We have a hard time finding meaning and motivation in work because we can't discover the meaning of our existence. When you know what your true self really wants, you can realize that the work you do is a precious opportunity and a means of expressing and realizing that self. And you will strive to express and realize yourself through that work.

When we are connected with ourselves, we can do the work we really want to do. If the work we're doing now is not what the true self wants, then we can challenge ourselves to find the work we want, or at least we can try to find meaning in the work that we've been given. Sometimes, you must do work just to make a living, which is not necessarily a problem. In that case, you can make an effort to create change, even in very small things. If you look carefully enough, you can find meaning in any situation. You can create little things that make a big difference in people's lives through your work, one day at a time, such as by having a positive attitude, opening your heart and smiling more, or trying to come up with creative ideas for the work you do. If we have a solid connection with ourselves, we never squander our energy, no matter where we are or what we are doing.

Work also feels hard if we're faced with a situation in which we have to accomplish a task that feels beyond our abilities. Those who are positive and filled with confidence will see this as an opportunity for personal growth, boldly taking on the challenge. Conversely, those who don't have this attitude, who are instead scared, will shirk from accepting the work. "This is beyond my abilities," they think. "How could I accomplish this? I absolutely cannot do it." Like the flea in the glass jar in Chapter 1, they *could* jump higher but don't even make the attempt. Determining their own limitations, they stay within the boundaries of their own expectations. "I can't do it. I can't go out of here. That's too hard and risky for me."

This passive, defensive attitude isn't limited to work. In various aspects of life, people bind themselves with fear. We need to realize that we ourselves are actually the ones creating that fear, imposing those limitations. It's a delusion, a virtual image we've created—a self-image. Breaking out of that image, like a chick breaking out of its shell, is the beginning of self-transformation and innovation. This is not something someone else can do for you. You must find the courage to face it yourself directly and shatter those images.

To draw out the power of the self-innovation, you must first meet and connect with it. You must enter your inner world, breaking the chain of your endless thoughts. You must throw back the illusory curtain of fear and limitation and encounter the essence of yourself, the light shining inside you.

Everything stated above in the last few pages might seem quite serious, and you might be tempted to deny that any of it applies to you. That is a possibility, but in reality some part of it is true for practically everyone. Making true and lasting changes in your life is not easy, and it requires being bluntly honest with yourself. Changing elements of your character is a little like weeding: you can just pull the stems off at the surface, or you can dig deeper and pull them out at the root. Only the latter will get rid of the problem for good.

As we have seen, when we look deeply into most of the problems that worry us, we realize that their causes and solutions are found in our connection to ourselves. If you are connected with your true self, you have nothing to fear in this world. With all the delusions surrounding you laid bare, you can feel yourself existing entirely between heaven and earth. That self isn't the self you used to know, but in your deep inner consciousness, it is the self you've always dreamed of and hoped for. You need to encounter that self. You need to connect with that self.

If you find yourself in a troubling or chaotic situation right now, don't blame your circumstances. Crisis, it has been said, is an opportunity. You may have the best opportunity to meet yourself. Growing distant from yourself, you suffer from confusion—which is bound to produce a fervent, do-or-die desire to escape from that distress. At such times, turn your eyes inward instead of finding fault in your abilities, your environment, or other people.

The more you understand the importance of connecting with your true self, the more you draw near to hope. "Yes, the problem was my disconnection from myself," you realize. Then, it's obvious what you should do next: reconnect with yourself!

"Connecting with myself is more important than anything else!" If this is how you feel, you're already starting to commune with yourself. Consider that attitude precious. And go within yourself; everything begins with *you*. No other life will be more meaningful, fulfilling, or moving, for you will be living as none other than your authentic true self.

CHAPTER 3

Find Solutions in the Unseen World

To connect with ourselves, we first have to uncover the reason for our disconnection. In the previous chapter, I said that we alienate ourselves from others and distance ourselves from ourselves because we fear failing and being rejected, which leads to disconnection. There's another fundamental reason, as well. We don't have a good connection with ourselves because our consciousness is mostly directed outward. To connect with ourselves, we have to turn our focus inward.

Most of the information we accept is from the outer "visible world," entering through our five senses. Information coming in through the visual sense, in fact, accounts for about 80 to 85 percent of that input. From the time we get up in the morning until we go to sleep at night, myriad bits of information come to us through our eyes. Try to imagine living for a day cut off from your visual sense. How hard and frustrating would that be? It would be difficult to take care of yourself in basic ways— to wash, get dressed, eat, and move, not to mention work.

For many of us these days, being cut off from our visual sense would feel like being completely disconnected from the world, since we're accustomed to fiddling with our smartphones all day, sending and receiving messages, never taking our eyes off our devices. Furthermore, people constantly make snap judgments about people and things based on how they look to us, deciding that one person is dangerous and another worthy of respect. Our consciousness is easily influenced by the visible world. So, to understand our own consciousness, we first need to understand the characteristics of the visible world.

Look around you. What do you see? Objects, people, nature— how do they look? Everything appears to be separate from everything else. You and others, nature itself, each look like discrete individuals and objects. Everything is disconnected in the world we see with our eyes. Separation and disconnection— these are characteristics of the visible world. So, in the structure of our consciousness, where information from the visible world dominates, everything is perceived and understood to be separate. In other words, we feel that we are separate from others, from the world.

When this consciousness that "I am separate from everything" encounters the ego, what sort of thinking does it lead to? "I'm alone," we feel. "The world is dangerous. There's no one in this harsh world to protect me. I have to protect myself." With such an awareness, each and every one of us is immersed in a game of survival. And rule number one for survival is this: "I have to be superior to others." A good school, a good job, a good record, a large salary, a wonderful spouse, a good house, a luxurious car, and other aspects of the visible world that establish our status in society become people's romantic fantasy.

In the game of survival, there are always winners and losers. Along with the bright smiles of the victorious minority are the tears of the failing, wounded, despairing losers. Yet we have to get up again, clutching our wounds and our painful memories of failure, to play this cutthroat game once again. Why? Because we have to survive. This is the naked face of the visible world we live in.

How great is the power of advertising and entertainment in the visible world to pull us in, getting us stuck in materialism and consumerism? Delicious food, beautiful clothing and accessories, luxurious cars, and new smartphones cause us to live with our attention completely captured by the outside world. These distractions are relentless, making us focus most of our conscious mind on dressing up and on purchasing shinier and and more fashionable stuff, instead of enriching ourselves internally. Without our realizing it, the visible world—a life based on comparisons to others—has taken its place as the central value of our lives. And many people are led about by this value in the way they think, make judgments, and live. Inevitably they grow distant and disconnected from their inner world.

Trained to chase the materialistic, external rewards offered by the world, such as money, success, and status, we gradually grow distant from our true selves. Though we may have many friends on social media, those we can open up to and share our hearts with are rare. Returning alone after dressing up and enjoying a noisy party, in one corner of our heart we feel emptiness rushing over us.

In most of the developed world, these are times of material plenty. Most people have enough to eat and a roof over their heads. Yet, people say they're not very happy. A growing number are depressed, confused, and anxious. That's how distant they have grown from themselves. They're disconnected from themselves, disconnected from others, and disconnected from nature. Impatient to have more, to climb higher, and to look cooler, people focus entirely on the visible world.

There's something we must understand here: no matter how much we focus on the outside, separation and disconnection are the defining characteristics of the visible world. Focusing on the outer world merely stimulates our desires and emotions even more. Only one method is available to us for recovering our connection with ourselves: We need to turn our outward-looking consciousness inward, concentrating on the invisible world, not the visible one.

So what then is the invisible world? It is the world detected through senses beyond the ordinary five. It's the world of consciousness, the world of energy. It is the foundation of who we are, the ground from which all transformation can occur.

To understand the invisible world, we must first understand that the universe is not made up of solid matter. Everything in this world is made up of energy. This statement is not merely my opinion; the work of quantum physicists has shown this to be true. Both solid, dense matter and empty-looking spaces are made up of energy. If we take any object and divide it again and again ever more microscopically to the particles that make up atoms, all that is left in the end is pure energy. Objects that seem separate and completely unrelated are actually different forms of the same energy.

All creation is made of the same energy, but it can be divided into the visible and invisible worlds, depending on the frequency of the energy. The visible, material world is made up of energy that has a slower frequency, while the energy in the invisible world has a very high frequency. For example, our physical bodies, which are visible, have low-frequency energy, while our unseen spirit—the world of consciousness—has a high, light-like frequency. Physicists are still looking to identify this "unified field," but traditional Asian medicine and philosophies view all types of energy as connected through primal cosmic energy. Reconnecting with this fundamental energy is the primary purpose and objective of Pineal Gland Meditation.

I have said that the fundamental cause of the many problems

we experience in life is our disconnection from ourselves. The reason for this disconnection is that we've focused solely on the visible world, which is characterized by separation and disconnection. Though we strive to find solutions in the visible world, we cannot help but reach conclusions that involve separation and disconnection. The more we concentrate on the visible world, the more our sense of separation and isolation grows.

The invisible world, on the other hand, is where we can find the ultimate solutions to our problems, for the nature of the invisible world is *connection and unity*. If you focus on the invisible world, you'll realize that matter and spirit, self and others, nature and humans are not separate from each other but interconnected by a single energy field. You'll move forward toward a consciousness of connection and unity, putting the sense of separation and disconnection behind you.

What, then, should you do to concentrate on the invisible world? It's all about taking your consciousness, an awareness focused on the visible world, and turning it inward instead.

The operation of our minds and our consciousness is truly amazing. Consciousness shrinks and shuts down tightly, only to expand without limit, becoming great enough to embrace the whole world. We can find solutions to our problems by using the characteristics of the mind, which is able to change and expand infinitely, to raise ourselves to a larger, higher, more luminous consciousness.

Anything humans do begins in the world of consciousness. When we make or do something, we first bring new thoughts or ideas to mind. Before making a delicious pasta meal for a helpful friend, for example, you first might think, "I should show her my gratitude." Or, before leaving on an impromptu trip, you first have the impulse to travel. Ideas and thoughts attract energy, turning it into matter and transforming it into reality.

What creates and moves the visible world, in fact, is the invisible world of consciousness.

Good news! Anyone can access these mysterious powers of consciousness. These functions are already installed in each of us, not somewhere far off. The problem is simply that many people don't know they have such functions within themselves, or if they do know, they're not familiar with how to use them. It's like having the latest smartphone but not really knowing what to do with it. Wouldn't it be helpful if we had a manual telling us how to apply our consciousness and our bodies and how to use energy well? The Pineal Gland Meditation you'll learn about in this book can play that role for you.

Another piece of good news! Connection and unity are part of our original nature. This isn't something new at all; once you understand, you'll realize that this has always been our true nature. All you have to do is return to that state. The goal of the Pineal Gland Meditation explained in this book is to enable you to *feel and live* this clear truth with your entire being, not simply understand it as knowledge.

As you've lived your life, you've already experienced that state of connection and unity. Think about your childhood, when you were still very small. You did not perceive the world as a place of separation back then. In your mother's arms, the world felt safe, and you had no worries at all. Weren't you endlessly joyful and happy when you played in nature? No doubt you experienced warm sunshine, lush flowers and trees, and starlight embroidering the night sky. Amid all that, hearts are full of a sense of abundance and connection, as if we are interconnected with everything, with no separation.

As we grow, however, that sense of connection and fullness gradually weakens. We feel inadequate somehow, lonely and empty, a gaping hole growing in our chest. We come to view the world from a different perspective, distinguishing ourselves from others and from the environment, our sense of ourselves as individual beings solidifying. Without quite realizing it, we slowly get used to a world where everything is separate and everyone is competing and calculating. We may even see others as competitors or dangers that threaten us.

The true nature you're born with is connection and unity, but the characteristics of the visible world—separation and discon-nection—create a sense of apartness, a massive gap inside you. It's safe to say that much of whatever suffering you experience derives from confusion from the disparity between your true nature and the reality you experience. While your original, true nature seeks connection and unity, your reality is far removed from that ideal. Could that be the source of all your troubles?

Where will you place your central values, in your true nature or in the reality you experience? It's a choice given to each of us. Will you continue to suffer in a consciousness of separation and disconnection? Or will you find peace and stability with an awareness of connection and unity? That decision is up to you, determining the direction of the great currents flowing through your life. In your heart, ask yourself this question: "What choice will allow me to escape suffering and find peace?" Then you'll feel the direction your heart really wants to go.

Listen to the voice of your true self. It wants to return to its original state—to reconnect, to be one, to go back to purity. The emptier and more frustrated you feel, the more the embers of longing glow at the bottom of your heart. Focus on those embers. Like a salmon returning to spawn, you will one day find your way home. That path leads back to the dwelling place of your soul, to who you truly are.

CHAPTER 4

An Ancient Map for Seeking Your Soul's Home

What is the substance of my true self, who I really am? The true self isn't some vague philosophical notion, to be pondered briefly and then ignored. It's a concrete feeling accessible to anyone. The true self exists in our hearts as *energy;* some call it the "soul." We can feel the energy of the soul clearly, use it in our daily lives, and share it with others.

Close your eyes and focus on your heart. Wait quietly to see what feelings you detect. When the energy of your soul is activated, you'll get the feeling of something expanding in your heart, like a gently moving and blooming feeling. That is the energy of your soul, your true self. If you feel nothing at all, or a stuffy feeling, that is also your soul's current energy state. I'll explain this in detail later, but your soul's energy feels that way when it's contracted by negative emotions. Don't worry, though. Energy is not fixed and unchanging. It can change at any time, depending on the condition of your body and mind. Later I'll lead you step by step through training for activating your soul energy.

It's not that difficult to encounter the substance of who you are. Soul energy unique to each person dwells within them.

That soul energy is the identity of each one of us. Amazing, isn't it, that people wander through life, searching for themselves, when what they seek is right inside them in their heart?

But here is one important thing you should be aware of now. The soul that you just felt in your heart is not all of the true self that you are looking for. Feeling the energy of the soul is just a starting point. Through the soul's journey, you will be able to feel your true identity as something much, much bigger and greater than you can imagine now. I hope you will discover what it is by the time you finish this book.

Life is viewed as a "journey of the soul" in the ancient Korean system of mind-body training called Sundo, which is the root source of the Pineal Gland Meditation I'll teach you. Sundo sees the soul as the center pervading everything from birth to death to what comes after. Sundo says that we have in our bodies a mysterious map that guides us through the birth, growth, and completion of the soul. This map includes three palaces and three gates.

You have probably heard of the chakras, a concept originating in the yogic traditions of India. The chakras are energy centers in the body that greatly impact our physical, mental, and spiritual well-being. The three palaces and three gates of Sundo are similar to the chakra system, but they contain a unique message regarding the birth, growth, and completion of the soul. I'll interpret for you—to the extent of my own realization and understanding—the ancient and mysterious map for the completion of the soul, and how our souls grow as they pass through these three palaces and three gates.

There was a place you stayed for a while before being born into this world: your mother's womb. As the first of Sundo's three palaces, the womb signifies the Earth Palace. The fetus grows here, receiving oxygen and nutrients from its mother.

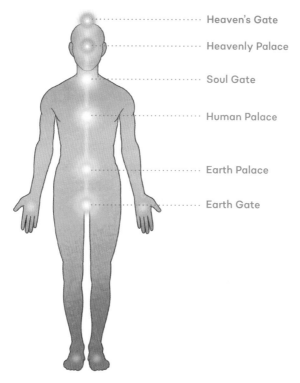

Heaven's Gate

Heavenly Palace

Soul Gate

Human Palace

Earth Palace

Earth Gate

Three Palaces and Gates in the Human Body

But at the moment of birth, the baby's body is not the only thing that is born. In fact, a soul is born into the world, temporarily borrowing a body to use as a vehicle on its earthly journey. However, accustomed to thinking only of the visible world, we usually only think about the mysteries of the body being born. But something even more miraculous has happened—a soul has begun its journey on earth. It's difficult to imagine a body without a soul, but our soul is the primary element of who we are, our body secondary. As a container holding the precious soul, the body acts as an assistant that helps the soul grow. How beautifully would a baby's soul grow if, based on this perception, we raised the child as a precious soul?

A baby coming out into the world passes through a gate as it emerges from its mother's body. In Korea, this gate is called the Jade Gate, signifying a woman's genitals. The first of the three gates, it is also called the Earth Gate—the gate through which a body comes into the world.

As a soul who has inhabited a body born into this world, imagine yourself as a newborn. The energy of your soul dwells in the heart of that gently sleeping baby. What was your soul's hope, coming to the earth? What goal did it have in choosing this journey? Each soul has some purpose it wants to fulfill. It's important to remember this. When you recognize yourself not merely as a body but as the soul dwelling in it, your soul's true desire will come to mind.

In Buddhism, they say that we are reborn to achieve something we failed to accomplish in a previous life. In this life, it is said, we get another opportunity to make up for something we regretted in a previous life. Whether or not you believe in past lives, aren't we all at least trying to lead lives we won't regret when we die?

Have you ever wondered what people regret most before they die? Do they regret not being richer? Do they regret not eating better food or wearing better clothes? No. I dealt with this subject in depth in my previous book, *I've Decided to Live 120 Years*. Surprisingly, the regrets most people have before dying are not about material things. They regret not living a life true to themselves. To put it another way, they regret failing to live up to the life desired by their true selves.

This fact should give you an inkling of how to live without regrets. Even if you try to live only for the material world, your soul will always be there in the background, urging you toward your higher calling in life. That's why living for the pleasures of the physical body leaves you feeling empty and alone. It is, of course, important to take care of your body and to enjoy your life on the earthly plane, but you have to have a clear idea of who your true self is and what it wants. To find this out, you must first connect to your true self.

Your true self is your soul, which dwells in your heart. In Sundo, the heart is called the Human Palace, the place that holds a person's true identity. This is the second palace.

To find out, then, what your soul wants to achieve through this life, ask your soul directly. Close your eyes and place one hand over the middle of your chest. Feel your breathing, along with the beating of your heart. With each breath and heartbeat, the energy of your soul is vitalized within your body. Try to feel your soul. That soul is *you*.

Try to feel the state of your soul's energy right now. It's enough to perceive the sensations in your chest. Does your chest feel light and tranquil, or is it frustrated and tight? Or is there no sensation at all? Whatever the feeling, that's the present energy state of your soul. What feelings do you want in your chest in the future? Do you want your chest to be warm and full? Do you want it to be free and light? Of course you do, because these are the sensations you feel when your soul is fulfilled and free. Everyone's soul energy wants to be free and light. It wants to love and be loved. It wants to commune with others. It wants to be joyful and peaceful. It's the nature of our souls to seek such an energy state.

To reach this state, the soul's energy needs to grow, expanding far and wide, not just remaining contracted in the heart. There is a definite goal and direction here. The soul's energy wants to change into more mature, purer energy so it can soar and transform into a higher level. It doesn't want to remain dark and heavy, as it exists when our mind is disconnected from it. In Sundo, this change sought by the soul's energy is called the "growth of the soul."

What should you do to let your soul energy grow? There is a

light that shines like a lighthouse to illuminate your soul's energy and to cause it to grow. This is the light of divinity. Anyone whose consciousness is elevated will encounter this bright light in their brain. It's called many things in diverse spiritual traditions—the source of life, divinity, God, heaven, nirvana, cosmic consciousness, the higher self, higher consciousness.

Our soul, our true nature, anxiously longs to encounter the divine, the true nature of the universe. Why? Because the true nature of the universe is the home of the soul. Like children longing for their mother, our true nature earnestly wants to be one with the true nature of the cosmos. This, in Sundo, is called *Shinin Hapil* (divine-human unity). *Shin* means "god," *in* means "human," *hap* means "to unite," and *il* means "one." Together, this means that the energy of the soul in the heart—the true identity of each human—encounters and becomes one with the light of divinity in the brain. Divine nature becoming human nature, God and humanity meeting as one, Shinin Hapil—this is the ultimate goal of Sundo training.

Shinin Hapil is not just a concept, but also a definite energy phenomenon arising in the brain and consciousness. The brain is the place where the soul's energy meets the light of divinity. That's why the brain is called the Heavenly Palace—the place where you meet with heaven, the place where heaven dwells. Through Pineal Gland Meditation, you can vividly experience the expanded energy of the soul in your heart rising to your head to become one with the light of divinity in your brain. Encountering heaven, all your loneliness and anxiety will be released, and the thirst of your soul will be quenched. With your whole body, heart, and mind, you experience complete unity, cosmos and self as one.

I use the term "heaven" quite a lot in this book, but the heaven I refer to may not match your idea of heaven, so I would like to clarify what I mean. The heaven that I refer to is not a specific "place" you go after death. Rather, it is the pure, celestial energy and consciousness we feel when we are connected with divinity. It's a state of energy and consciousness. In other words, it's what I used to call "cosmic energy, cosmic mind."

Anyone can experience Shinin Hapil. Sufficient preparation is needed, though. Just as water's boiling point, 100 degrees Celsius, is a universal phenomenon of energy, the energy of our souls encountering the light of divinity is a phenomenon that occurs when the principles of energy are satisfied. To boil water, we have to keep applying heat. In the same way, to make the soul energy in your heart rise to the Heavenly Palace in your brain, you have to keep causing it to grow, making it mature and pure. This means opening your heart more, being more positive, more tolerant, more loving, more giving. Then the energy of your soul can escape from its selfish condition and mature to a place of plenty where it can embrace all things.

On its way to the Heavenly Palace, there is a gate through which the energy of the soul must pass. This is the Soul Gate, located in the neck area—the second gate spoken of in Sundo. To pass through this gate, the energy of the soul must meet sufficient conditions. It must become pure, like the spirit of a young child, and mature, like the loving heart of a mother. This is not easy, though, the gate being like the "narrow door" spoken of in the Bible (Luke 13:22–30). Yet, it is possible, if you commit yourself to doing so. Later in this book, I will give you detailed guidance on how you can make the soul's energy pure and mature.

The third and final gate remains—Heaven's Gate, the gateway to heaven. It is in the crown of the head, the highest part of the human body. This is also the location of an energy point where the energy of heaven enters the body. If you've ever touched the crown of a baby's head, you'll know that the point is soft, throbbing up and down with the child's heartbeat. Heavenly energy easily enters through Heaven's Gate during infancy because the bones in the child's head haven't completely fused, but this connection weakens as they grow and the skull closes.

Most people live without knowing of Heaven's Gate, where heavenly energy enters their bodies. However, through meditation or energy training, we can feel the life energy of heaven coming down into this place when it is open. Heaven's Gate is a crucial place for us to experience being connected with heavenly energy and at one with cosmic consciousness. That's why in Korean culture, not just anyone was allowed to touch the crown of another person's head, and if someone was lying down, people weren't supposed to walk past the crown of their head. This custom reflects consideration for others, ensuring that their connection with the energy of heaven isn't broken.

Sundo considers the moment of death to be of primary importance, since this is the moment of the soul's passage through Heaven's Gate. The energy of the soul arriving in our bodies when we are born leaves at the moment of death. If the soul has finished its journey of completion, it may then leave through the crown of the head, uniting with the energy of heaven. In Sundo, this is called *Chunhwa*, "becoming heaven." *Chun* indicates "heaven" and *hwa* means "become." Referring to the death of a completed soul, Chunhwa is the highest level of death spoken of in Sundo.

By connecting with the energy of heaven, our souls achieve completion. The key to Sundo training is living with a consciousness that is as bright and clear as heaven itself until, when your life ends, you return to the world of bright and clear energy. Completion of the soul—this is the true purpose for which our souls have come into the world.

What do you think? Do you understand the meaning of the three palaces and three gates in our bodies, of the process of life from birth to death called the "journey of the soul"? If we only focus on the material world, our lives are just our bodies being born, growing, aging, getting sick, and dying. In all life's craziness, we eat and drink, love and hate, laugh and cry, and rush this way and that, pushed by the body's needs, pulled by life's emotional ups and downs. But when we center our view on the unseen world, we realize that this whole process is a journey for the growth of our souls. It's a process through which our souls borrow a body and are born, entering the world for the purpose of learning and growing through all kinds of suffering and conflict, joy and love.

Each of us has things to learn and awaken to in this world. If you have a problem right now, one that is making life uniquely hard and worrisome for you, try thinking of it as a special assignment that heaven has given you. Even the Bible says, "Heaven will not let us be tried beyond what we can bear" (1 Corinthians 10:13). The energy of your soul will grow in the process of solving your problems and dealing with the circumstances you face. You may taste joy, but you may also experience pain. Discard any thought that you should expect only joy in life. Don't curse the presence of conflict in your life, for it is your invitation to grow. You can never grow if you just curl up, afraid of the pain that comes from confrontation. Like lotuses growing in the mud, our souls are able to bloom beautifully through pain.

Joy or pain, welcome it all. Spread your arms wide, making your heart large enough to embrace all of life's suffering and pleasure. Be grateful that you have been given problems to solve and the space and time in which you can solve them bit by bit, running up against your ego, other people, and the world. Be grateful that your heart and soul are always present—right now, in this moment. These gifts are all here for you and for the growth of your soul.

If you look at everything from the soul's perspective, you'll gradually begin to understand its hidden principles. You'll see that you have come to this place for the growth and completion of your soul, and that other people, too, whether they know it or not, have come with the same mission in their hearts. Here and now, in these times, we are companions, fellow travelers on the journey of the soul.

CHAPTER 5

Ancient Practices for Connecting with Yourself

Did you know that nature already contains everything you need to know about life? You may have noticed that plants and animals don't have to think much about their lives to live successfully. So long as they have basic necessities, like food and safety, they can thrive. Stress diseases are a uniquely human trait, a problem brought about entirely by the human mind. You could say that we overthink to the point of disconnecting ourselves from the natural rhythms of life.

When Sundo masters practiced their craft, they usually did so while living in the lush mountains of Korea. Here, they could be in direct contact with nature, and their principles of energy thus developed in accord with the natural laws that govern the universe. When we modern people lose connection with ourselves, it is because we have also lost connection with these natural principles.

Fortunately, Sundo not only has a map for the completion of the soul, made up of the three palaces and three gates described in the previous chapter, but also concrete principles and practices that let us directly experience this map step by step to achieve completion based on natural principles.

A record of this is found in the *Sam Il Shin Go,* one of Korea's three ancient scriptures of Sundo. It teaches about five topics: the universe, God, heaven, the world, and truth. Three practices—*Jigam, Joshik,* and *Geumchok*—are included in its teachings on truth.

The first practice, Jigam, is literally translated as "stopping emotion." In Korean, *ji* means "to stop" and *gam* means "emotion." The *Sam Il Shin Go* mentions six kinds of human emotion—joy, fear, sadness, anger, greed, and dislike—and says that you can arrive at truth only if you stop those emotions.

It's easy to lose a sense of our true selves when we're swept away in a whirlpool of feelings. Consider this situation as an example. A businessman has to commute 45 minutes to the office each day. The highway is crowded with aggressive drivers, all trying to get to work as quickly as possible. Inevitably, someone cuts him off or tailgates him. His anger and frustration builds. He curses or honks his horn, but that offers little relief. He arrives at the office, straightens his jacket and tie, and walks in the door. His emotions are now below the surface, but only barely.

If uncontrolled, such a pattern of emotion can become habitual. Our emotional patterns then become part of our perceived personality, and we imagine that they are part of who we are. But is that anger who you are? No, it's not. You always have the ability to choose your emotions, if you are willing to develop the discipline to do so. Your emotions *belong to* you; they're not who you really *are.* But overwhelmed by waves of feelings, you mistake your emotions for yourself. You speak and act emotionally because in that moment you have lost your real self.

What should you do to come back to who you really are? You must silence the emotions that have held you captive. To do that, you have to be able to observe your emotions dispassionately and separate your true self from the energy of those emotions. This is more easily said than done, you may think. But with the right training tools, it is possible. Jigam is a training method that lets you stop your emotions and easily return to your true self as your emotional energy subsides and you feel pure energy moving through your body. I'll provide you with detailed guidance on Jigam training in Chapter 7.

The second of the three Sundo practices, Joshik, is "breath control." *Jo* means "make even or regular" and *shik* means "breath." Try to remember how you've breathed when you've been angry. You probably took hard, short, rough breaths. Conversely, how is your breathing when your body and mind are calm and comfortable? Your breaths are probably slow and peaceful. Breathing reflects the state of your energy.

The *Sam Il Shin Go* categorizes six energy states according to breathing: full energy, blocked energy, cold energy, hot energy, dry energy, and wet energy. Not everybody has the same type of energy. For example, some people have a lot of water energy, cold and wet, while others have lots of fire energy, hot and dry. If you have a great deal of water energy, you'll have many thoughts and worries, making your energy heavier and stagnant. With a lot of fire energy, you'll tend to show anger easily, and you'll be unable to control your temper. I'm not saying that either water energy or fire energy is bad. Expressed positively, water energy manifests in flexibility and sociability, fire energy in passion and vitality. But nothing excessive is good. If you have too much of something, getting rid of some of it is the best approach. You should balance things by discharging excess energy from your body.

Aren't you curious about how you can discharge excess energy from your body when you can't see it with your eyes or touch it with your hands? The best method for doing this is breathing, Joshik. This may sound simplistic, but those who do energy training and meditation find that breathing is the most powerful way to balance your body's energy and to elevate your consciousness.

We experience the effect of breathing in our daily lives, though we may be unaware of it. When you're angry or frustrated, what do you do to resolve these feelings? Don't you exhale, in a deep sigh, "Hoo . . . ," sending out the stifling energy in your chest? Though we've never been taught how to do this, our bodies are made to react this way automatically. We breathe out the excess emotional energy in our bodies. In this way, we escape from the emotions that have trapped us, allowing us to return to our original state of balance, reconnecting with ourselves. What's more, through breath control we continuously boost the fresh, clear energy in our bodies, increasing our vitality and raising ourselves to a brighter, clearer awareness.

The third Sundo practice, Geumchok, is "prohibiting contact." The six stimuli mentioned in the *Sam Il Shin Go* are sounds, colors, smells, tastes, lust, and touch. These constantly turn our awareness outward. Try to calculate how much of your day is spent with your attention turned outward and how much with it turned inward, quietly connecting with yourself. Some are in the habit of connecting with themselves, and some strive in their own way to do this. But many people would say that they don't spend even 10 minutes doing this.

For most of the day, from when we get up in the morning until we go to bed at night, our attention is turned outward. We are watching, listening, talking, eating, or touching most of the time. And these days, people often lose themselves in their smartphones, TVs, and computers all day, fatiguing their eyes. With their brains connected to the information coming in through those screens, even while eating and walking, they ignore their connection with their inner world.

If our senses are focused on the outside, we naturally grow distant from our inner world and disconnect from ourselves. We laugh and cry in response to what we see in the outside world, forgetting who we are. And, in turn, we mistake such thoughts and emotions for who we are. To reconnect with ourselves, we must turn our attention inward. This means prohibiting contact, Geumchok, or focusing entirely within. In this case, "within" means our body and our true selves.

In the *Sam Il Shin Go*, these three practices—Jigam, Joshik, and Geumchok—are said to be methods for "reflecting on delusion to arrive at truth." The visible world constantly deludes us because it makes everything appear separate and disconnected. Thus, we are constantly perplexed by illusions and misunderstandings. At such times, try closing your eyes and quietly practicing Jigam, Joshik, and Geumchok. By stopping your emotions, controlling your breathing, and focusing entirely within, you can experience your inner eyes opening and all the delusional images around you disappearing. Things that once seemed separate and disconnected may now start connecting and merging.

It's been about 40 years since I started teaching traditional mind-body practices based on Sundo to the world. What I've been doing is helping people reconnect with themselves. I've helped them connect with their bodies and discover who they really are, and I've guided them so they can escape from the limits of their small selves and grow into their big selves. For this I took the Sundo practices of Jigam, Joshik, and Geumchok, which are designed to help people control and direct energy, and I adapted them for modern times. I have taught these practices as the methods of Body & Brain Yoga and Brain Education. Whatever these methods are called, at their heart they are exactly the same. In short, they exist to help people connect with themselves. The bottom line is that it always comes back to you.

The path we walk in life is beset by innumerable problems. The world is full of advice and methods, and many people make confident claims that they know the secret to solve our problems. "This idea will really change your life," they may say. "Try this method. It'll make you healthy and happy." "Look at this totally new technology, which is on a completely different level from what's gone before." We are appealed to with all kinds of ideas and approaches.

But how well have external advice and methods solved your problems so far? They probably haven't helped that much, or served only as a temporary fix. How, then, can you really solve those problems? To solve a problem, you need to find its root cause. It seems obvious to me that one simple thing lies at the heart of all our troubles. As I've already stressed, they all originate in our disconnection from ourselves. That's why, to resolve a problem, the most important thing is to authentically reconnect with yourself. When you connect with yourself, you know and are able to manage yourself. Instead of just living however things work out, or being a spectator to your own life, you can live an authentic life as the true master of yourself.

Recovery of the broken connection with yourself is at the heart of the Pineal Gland Meditation you will learn about in this book. That work will proceed in three steps. The first step is *connecting with your body*, the second is *connecting with your soul*, and the third is *connecting with your divinity*. It's about focusing *inside* the body, discovering your true self and growing into your higher self. I've combined in these three steps the simple but essential core of the methods I've been teaching, based on the Sundo practices of Jigam, Joshik, and Geumchok.

Focusing within is most important for connecting with yourself—to begin the work of illuminating and exploring your inner world, your consciousness. After focusing for a while on your invisible, internal world, you will feel your inner world gradually brightening and your understanding growing. You will develop a new eye for seeing the previously unseen world.

This "sixth sense" is commonly called the third eye, the spiritual eye, the mind's eye, or the all-seeing eye. The eye we're talking about here is not the physical eye. Rather, it is bright consciousness. It speaks of the power to see with insight into the currents and principles of the unseen world, moving from an awareness once focused on the visible world. It's the eye of wisdom opening, the mind's eye seeing through to previously invisible principles. It enables you to see things more broadly, deeply, and clearly than before.

Ordinarily, when we see phenomena arising, we make judgments based only on what we see. Seeing the outwardly visible world, it is impossible to completely understand the principles by which you, others, and the world work unless you can see the principles operating beyond the scenes. Those principles of the invisible world are the actions of consciousness, the operations of energy. What we see with our eyes came about because consciousness and energy acted first.

To understand the principles of the unseen world of consciousness and energy, you must first understand what consciousness and energy are and how they operate. You can experience this through Pineal Gland Meditation. You can explore and illuminate the world using energy as a tool that is felt throughout your body and mind.

Our bodies are energy, and our minds (our consciousness) are energy, too. To make your body healthy and your mind bright, simply train your energy through your body and mind. To make your body healthy, that's enough to train your energy, smoothly circulating it in your body, strengthening your vital energy. To make your mind bright, cleanse the dark aspects of your mind and release your dark energy, making your energy bright. Once you grasp these principles, you'll find that it's actually simple to put your mind and body in a state of wellbeing and to keep them there. As their masters, we can change and manage our bodies and minds instead of being controlled by them.

Everything in the universe must follow the principles of nature, or it is doomed to failure. Our bodies and minds, after all, are part of nature. The point of Pineal Gland Meditation is to properly understand the principles of nature inside us and to act according to those principles in order to manifest our authentic selves. It's about accessing the functions that have always been in our bodies and brains. To do this, we need to understand the natural principles and functions latent in our bodies. Sundo calls this the human energy system, and it provides three steps for human energy development.

Key aspects of the human energy system are the three major energy centers of the body. The first is in the abdomen, the second in the chest, and the third in the brain. These are the three palaces—Earth Palace, Human Palace, and Heavenly Palace—described in Chapter 4. You can imagine the palace as a rounded shape, like a ball. Condensed energy collects at these sites, which are called *dahnjons*—*dahn* meaning "energy" and *jon* meaning "field." The energy center in your abdomen is the lower dahnjon, the energy center in your chest is the middle dahnjon, and the energy center in your brain is the upper dahnjon. The three energy centers affect each other as they operate ceaselessly in our bodies.

Right now, try to feel the energy centers operating in your body. First, try to feel the lower dahnjon in your abdomen, at a point about two inches below the navel and two inches inside.

Upper Dahnjon

Middle Dahnjon

Lower Dahnjon

Three Energy Centers

The energy in the lower dahnjon is called *jung*, and it is red in color and hot in character. Imagine bright embers glowing red in the furnace of your lower dahnjon, emitting warm heat and light. Jung energy controls our physical health. Generally, the main point of physical training is to strengthen the abdominal core because this spot is closely related to the vital energy of the body.

Are you curious about the condition of your jung energy? You can assess it based on its relative density. When your jung energy is full, your lower abdomen will be warm, you will have good digestion, and you will overflow with vitality. Even your hands and feet, the parts of your body farthest from the center, will be warm, since blood and energy are circulating well throughout your body. When people have low levels of physical vitality, or weak digestive or reproductive systems, it's because the energy of their lower dahnjon is weak and their lower abdomen cold.

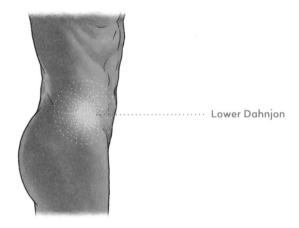

.... Lower Dahnjon

Energy System in the Lower Dahnjon

They have cold hands and feet because the warm energy of their core doesn't circulate all the way to their extremities. Unless you're charged with jung energy, you will have poor energy circulation and activity throughout your body.

The very first step in Sundo training is to charge yourself with jung energy, strengthening your core. This state of charged jung energy is called *Jungchoong* in Korean, *jung* meaning "physical energy" and *choong* meaning "full" or "packed." This is the first level you need to master for Pineal Gland Meditation, and the first step toward *connecting with your body*.

Next try concentrating on your chest. That's where the energy center called the middle dahnjon is located. Activating the energy of your chest is the second step of Pineal Gland Meditation, *connecting with your soul*. The middle dahnjon is in the very middle of your chest, centered on the energy point midway between the nipples. The energy in the middle dahnjon, called *ki* (or *qi/chi*), is yellow or green in color, and is a comfortable temperature, neither too hot nor too cold. The standard for determining the degree of your ki activation is clarity (clear versus cloudy). The purer and maturer the energy of this place, the better.

Have you ever experienced a feeling of comfort and openness in your chest? Try to remember what your breathing was like then, and what the expression on your face was like. Your breathing was probably comfortable, your facial expression cheerful, a gentle smile lifting the corners of your mouth. Conversely, there will have been times when you had a stifling feeling of blockage in your chest. What was your facial expression then? You probably wore a frown without realizing it and had trouble breathing comfortably. This happens when the energy in the chest is blocked so that it doesn't circulate properly and its purity is degraded, making it cloudy.

Why does the ki energy in the chest become clearer or cloudier? Two kinds of energy, of the soul and of emotion, coexist in our chest. The soul's energy is pure and positive, like love and compassion. Emotions, on the other hand, are more variable. Ideally, one becomes the master of one's emotions and is able to maintain a state of equanimity that resonates with the peace and tranquility of the soul. But, for most people, this requires training and the development of self-discipline. The energy of emotion is often cloudy and negative, holding on to resentment, anger, and jealousy. Other times, it might be positive, but overly excited, which leaves the mind unfocused.

The emotional confusion we feel comes from a battle between the energies of emotion and the energies of the soul. When one increases, the other decreases. The more the energy of the soul is activated, the more the energy of emotion decreases and the easier you can manage it. Conversely, if emotional energy takes control of our hearts, the energy of the soul contracts.

There's an expression that Koreans use when they lose confidence: "My ki has died." This phrase expresses a condition of the heart in which ki energy has contracted. But what about when your ki has revived? You overflow with confidence, and your body exudes bright, powerful energy. In this state, the soul has revived and negative emotions have decreased. But when the opposite happens, when your ki has "died," your confidence hits the floor, enveloping you in all kinds of negative feelings. If your emotions win the struggle for mastery, your soul energy gradually contracts, disabling it. When emotional energy totally conquers soul energy, we misidentify ourselves, thinking that we are our emotions, and our connection with our soul is broken.

During the second step of Pineal Gland Meditation, you will prioritize activating the energy center in your chest, the middle dahnjon. The goal is to revive the energy of the soul as you begin to restore connection with it. In Sundo, this process is called *Kijang*. Here *ki* means "ki energy" and *jang* means "to mature" or "to grow." Mature means that the power to control and regulate the energy of your ego and emotions increases, and the understanding and tolerance of yourself and others is expanded.

Once jung energy in the lower dahnjon becomes full, the energy of the middle dahnjon is naturally activated. That's why people whose lower dahnjon is charged, their bodies overflowing with vitality, tend to be more open-minded, active, and positive than those whose lower energy center is not charged. Fortunately, once you attain Jungchoong, it's easy to achieve Kijang. The energy of one step causes a chain reaction, like a domino effect. Thus, the soul energy of the activated middle dahnjon will also activate energy in the upper dahnjon—so once you attain Kijang, it's easy to reach the final step of brightening divinity. The soul energy activated in the chest rises to the head, awakening the energy of the upper dahnjon. It is called *Shinmyung*. *Shin* means "shin energy" or "divinity," and *myung* means "bright."

When the vital energy of the lower dahnjon is strengthened through Jungchoong and the soul energy of the middle dahnjon matures through Kijang, the energy of the upper dahnjon naturally shines brighter. Based on these principles of human energy development—Jungchoong, Kijang, and Shinmyung—you can awaken your pineal gland, naturally and effectively, without any side effects.

But if you concentrate on your head to awaken your pineal gland immediately without this process of preparation, your energy will suddenly rush to your head. For an ideal energy balance, your head should be cool and your abdomen warm. But when energy rushes to your head, this balanced state is reversed. Your abdomen, which should be warm, is cooled, and your head, which should be cool, grows hot. If this happens to you, a severe headache or a sense of pressure may develop in your head, and you may feel nauseous or dizzy, or even experience visual or other hallucinations. These are negative side effects that people may experience when they start Pineal Gland Meditation without proper preparation.

Those with a weak lower dahnjon or core will be more susceptible to such symptoms. To prevent that, you need to strengthen the energy in your core to make it full and strong. The condensed and grounded energy in your abdomen plays the role of an anchor to bring your thinking and emotional energy down to your lower dahnjon.

Problems also develop when the middle dahnjon isn't activated. Occasionally the spiritual eye of a very sensitive person will open suddenly, without any preparation, and that person may develop special abilities, such as seeing auras or past lives. However, if the energy of the person's middle dahnjon isn't pure, it's easy for them to be arrogant about those abilities or to misuse them to control others for the purpose of satisfying their own selfish desires. If the energy in your heart is pure and mature, you'll feel great joy in your soul when you use your spiritual abilities to help others. So it's crucial that before activating your pineal gland, you go through a process of preparation by first cleansing and purifying the emotional energy in your chest.

Now, let's move on to the last step, Shinmyung. Try to concentrate your mind on your brain, where the energy center called the upper dahnjon is located. The pineal gland is one part of the upper dahnjon energy system. Working only on the pineal gland itself, as an anatomical organ, is not enough to awaken it. Only when the entire system of the upper dahnjon operates smoothly will the pineal gland, its center, awaken. The energy system of the upper dahnjon is made up of many energy points in the head. The shin energy in the upper dahnjon has a bright navy blue or indigo color, taking on a violet or colorless bright light as you go up to the crown of the head.

To determine the degree of shin energy activation, you can check the brightness of that energy. Expressions like "your consciousness is bright" or "your consciousness is dark" describe precise characteristics of shin energy. If the shin energy is bright, then your consciousness brightens, too, and if your shin energy is dark, then your consciousness also dims.

What are people with bright consciousness like? They have wisdom, intuition, and insight. Their faces and eyes shine. Bright shin energy in the brain is usually described as a kind of light. In paintings of saints, including those of the Buddha and Jesus, this enlightened state is expressed by halos drawn around the figures' heads. Attaining this illuminated state of shin energy is the third step of Pineal Gland Meditation, *connecting with your divinity.*

Reaching this state of Shinmyung means seeing the world through enlightened consciousness. That's utterly different from gaining special abilities such as reading the thoughts or feelings of others or seeing past lives or people's auras, having been born with psychic senses, or randomly developing them. Seeing or not seeing something mystical isn't what's important. Such things are energy phenomena, like the side branches on a tree. What's important is knowing the essence, the root. This means seeing the world through an integrated consciousness of unity, in which everything is interconnected as one.

Such enlightenment comes when your soul encounters the light of divinity in your brain, when your true nature is one with the true nature of the cosmos. If you truly want to grow your soul, cultivate an earnest, passionate desire to encounter the light of divinity. That desire is the longing of your soul, welling up from a place deep in your heart. It is the longing to transcend the limits of your imperfect self, experiencing wholeness in the light of divinity. Embrace and develop that earnest longing in your heart. The more you live according to that longing, the closer you will draw to your true nature and the true nature of the cosmos.

PART II

Pineal Gland Meditation

CHAPTER 6

Connecting with Your Body

Who is your closest friend? You might think of the people coming in and out of your life when answering this question, but maybe your best friend is always with you on this journey. Personally, I consider my body to be my closest friend, my best buddy, since it is always there for me and is my greatest asset through the process of life. While my soul is my substance, my body is the precious vessel and vehicle containing that soul. Without bodies, our souls cannot affect material reality. It is because they have bodies that our souls can interact with other people and things—experiencing, feeling, expressing, creating, and growing.

The body is truly the partner of the soul. Our souls are contained within our bodies 24 hours a day, never apart for even a second. You are always enmeshed with it, but you don't really spend much time concentrating solely and entirely on your body. Your consciousness is focused outward most of the time, or immersed in thoughts of your own making.

Have you ever seen an image of some delicious-looking ice cream on TV and then had that image stick in your head, refusing to leave? Have you ever spent a lot of time thinking about whether to buy some clothes you saw on a home shopping network or on the internet? Countless bits of external information enter through your eyes, ears, nose, mouth, and skin, constantly stirring up thoughts and feelings inside you. Your ability to focus on your body drops as busy thoughts whirl around in your head. Your mind spins only in your head, unable to come down into your body. That separates your body and head, disconnecting your mind from your body.

Why is connecting with the body important? Our soul exists in our body—or, to be more precise, in our chest. To connect with the soul in our heart, our mind must come into our body, not wander around outside it. A process for becoming mindful of the body, the container of the soul, must come first. That's why connecting with your body is the first step of Pineal Gland Meditation.

Connecting with your body means calling your awareness into your body by focusing entirely on your body. There are many different methods for doing this, like walking or exercising by consciously moving the body as in yoga, tai chi, or qigong. Even during such practices, it's easy for your mind to be directed outward; you look at the scenery or other people, or think about this and that.

I've devised many training methods and movements for connecting with the body. I'll introduce a few of them here—those I consider the simplest and most effective. One of these is Toe Tapping. Lying in a comfortable position, you repeat the motion of tapping your feet together to make a rapping sound. Another is Belly Button Healing, which involves using a tool or your fingers to repeatedly press your navel. These movements are so simple that you can learn them in a minute, but within their simplicity are hidden profound principles.

For both of these exercises you repeat simple motions, creating a frequency. Nothing is more effective than vibrational frequencies for calming a brain filled by continuous, buzzing thoughts, and for calling awareness into the body.

You have probably experienced this in your daily life. What do you do to put a baby to sleep? You hold it in your arms while bouncing it gently up and down, pat it rhythmically on the chest with the palm of your hand, or rock its cradle. Those repetitive motions create comfortable vibrations. At some point the once-crying baby falls asleep.

And this works for grown-ups, too. Have you ever sat in a rocking chair, your mind gradually growing calmer as you rocked back and forth? Or sometimes, when your mind is anxious and impatient, you shake your legs without even realizing it, or stand up and pace back and forth. Such repetitive movements help relax your tension and release your anxious thoughts and feelings. Amazingly, our bodies do these things automatically. That's probably because we were created so that our bodies and brains are automatically relaxed by comfortable, repetitive vibrations.

To understand these phenomena, let's look at the structure of our brains for a moment. There are different ways to describe brain structure, and neurology is a complex and growing scientific discipline, but a simple way to understand its overall structure is to divide the brain into three basic tiers.

The outermost cerebral cortex generally supervises thinking, and the limbic system below it generally supervises emotion. The brainstem, at the centermost part of the brain, is the life brain, supervising essential vital functions such as breathing, heartbeat, and blood pressure through the sympathetic and parasympathetic nervous systems. The pineal gland is located here.

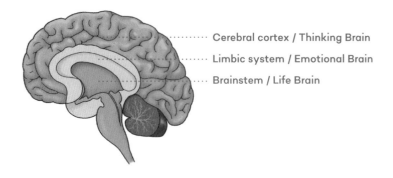

Cerebral cortex / Thinking Brain

Limbic system / Emotional Brain

Brainstem / Life Brain

Three-Layer Structure of the Brain

It is when your awareness remains mainly outside your life brain that you get stuck in thoughts and emotions. Comfortable, repetitive vibrations have the effect of calming the thinking and emotional brain as it calls your awareness into the life brain. Then naturally breathing becomes more comfortable and heart rate and blood pressure more stable.

Toe Tapping and Belly Button Healing have another thing in common besides repetitive vibration, and that's breathing. Vibrate repetitively for a while, and before you know it you'll find yourself exhaling through your mouth. By repeatedly tapping your toes or pressing your belly button, you'll discover that you're continuously exhaling the energy that had stagnated inside you, stifling you—the energy of thought and emotion. You can discharge the cold, hot, dry, and wet energy in your body. That is breath control, Joshik, introduced in Chapter 5.

Joshik happens in two stages when you do these exercises. The first stage is discharging the energy of thought and emotion by exhaling while you repeat the movements. After driving out your body's stagnant energy this way, you replenish yourself with clear, clean energy. That is the second stage of Joshik: after completing all the movements, you control your breathing.

For example, after doing Toe Tapping while lying down, stop right where you are. Spend some time exhaling, discharging stagnant energy through your mouth. After your energy is cleansed to some extent, start slowly controlling your breath, making it smooth, even, and deep. It's amazing how comfortable and deep breathing becomes now. You'll feel, "Oh, so this is what breathing naturally is like!" Thoughts and emotions grow calm, and you start to feel life itself through the vital phenomena occurring within you. And you'll experience what it means for your mind to stay completely in your body. This is the first step of Pineal Gland Meditation, connecting with your body.

Toe Tapping

It's fine to do this exercise in a sitting posture if you want to keep it simple, but you'll experience deeper relaxation and Joshik by doing it while lying down.

Lie in a comfortable position with your back on the floor, and close your eyes. Spread your arms a little apart from your trunk; open your hands, palms facing up. With your legs touching, tap your feet together so that they make a rapping sound. Focus your mind in your toes. Energy will sink down into your toes when you focus on them in accordance with the principle of energy: where the mind goes, energy follows. This is a method for letting your brain relax, providing relief from its tangle of thoughts. Continue exhaling through your mouth, expelling the stagnant, cloudy energy of thoughts and emotions. This has the effect of cleaning and purifying your body's energy through exhalation, like turning on a fan to expel stagnant air from a room.

After doing about 100 toe taps, rest for a minute. It's important to focus on exhaling, visualizing stagnant energy leaving your body through the tips of your toes. You'll actually get a

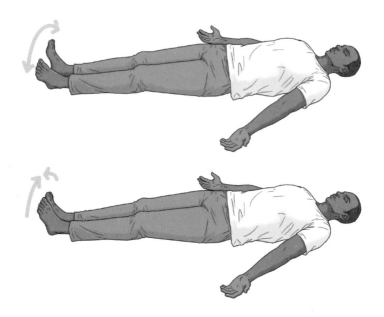

tingling feeling in your toes and a sense of heavy energy leaving your body through the tips of your toes. The energy points in our fingers and toes act as gates through which energy can enter or exit the body.

Repeat this process for at least five sets of 100 toe taps. Each time you go on to the next set, visualize stagnant energy leaving from higher up in your body. For example, when you do the second set, imagine stagnant energy from your thighs and hips leaving through your toes; when you do the third set, from your lower back and abdomen; for the fourth set, from your chest; and for the fifth set, from your head and entire body.

Depending on your condition, five sets may be enough, or you may have to do a few more sets. It's good to keep doing sets until your chest feels comfortable and light. The more heavy energy that leaves, the lighter your body will feel.

What happens after you do several sets of toe tapping is even more important. In that state, without moving, begin the second stage of Joshik. With your eyes closed, focus your mind on your body. Your body will feel light after the stagnant energy has left it through your toes. Now visualize your energy point in the crown of your head opening as the clear, pure energy of heaven enters through it. Imagine energy passing from your head to your chest, abdomen, and legs, cleaning out any remaining stagnant energy and sending it out through the tips of your toes. Your whole body, from your head to your toes, is now connected as a single energy field. Your body will feel truly light, like a floating cloud.

Observe your breathing. You'll be able to feel that your breathing has become very comfortable and deep, effortless. It feels like heavenly energy is breathing for you, coming in and out of your body, infusing you with pure, refreshing energy. Life is breathing, and you are life itself. Your whole consciousness fills your body. You and your body are completely connected. You'll feel, "The breath comes in and goes out all by itself like this! I exist like this, right now. This is life!" Feel completely one with your body, and experience your body as a manifestation of life itself, here and now, in this moment. Try to feel this as you do the exercise.

You can do Toe Tapping at any time, but it's most effective before going to sleep. Through this exercise, you can send out all the energy of fatigue that has built up in your body and mind during the day, replacing it with clear, fresh energy. And your brain waves will slow to a state of semi-sleep, allowing you to enter deep sleep immediately. Toe Tapping is the best exercise for summoning sweet dreams.

Belly Button Healing

The next exercise is Belly Button Healing. People tend to think of the belly button as simply a scar from when their umbilical cord was cut at birth. As I was developing different healing methods, though, I came to have great interest in the navel.

Pressing and massaging my navel, I discovered that my breathing deepened, the condition of my intestines improved, and energy and blood circulation throughout my body got better. These truly amazing and diverse effects were possible because around the navel are major organs for maintaining vital functions such as digestion, circulation, breathing, and immunity. Through Belly Button Healing, you can help promote these bodily activities. I'll give you a brief introduction here, but for detailed information, please see my book, *Belly Button Healing*.

There's a saying in Eastern medicine: "When the intestines are clear, the brain is clear." This saying reflects how essential intestinal health is for overall well-being, including that of the brain. The functions of the intestines and the brain are closely connected through what is known as the gut-brain axis. The main avenue of connection is the vagus nerve—the longest, most widely distributed cranial nerve, which bypasses the spinal cord to connect directly with the brainstem. Has your stomach ever hurt or have you ever had digestive problems when you were stressed or heard bad news? Have you ever had a headache when you had gas in your intestines or were constipated? These examples show the close relationship of the intestines with the brain.

In itself, however, the digestive system is so important for maintaining life that it has its own nervous system, the enteric nervous system, or "gut brain," which operates semi-independently of the brain. Like the brain, the enteric nervous system has cells that accept and process information and issue commands to digestive organs. It continues its activity when disconnected from the brain or even in a state of brain death.

Through the communication of these two important "brains," our intestines also affect our emotional state. Nerve cells, intestinal wall cells, and bacterial cells in the intestines secrete over 95 percent of our body's serotonin, a neurotransmitter giving us a feeling of well-being, and 50 percent of our dopamine, a neurotransmitter giving us feelings of happiness. Depression and anxiety have been linked to intestinal problems. Improving your gut health may increase your secretion of serotonin, contributing to a positive mood and feelings of satisfaction and ambition.

Belly Button Healing may improve gut and brain function because repetitively pressing the belly button massages the intestines that lie beneath it. The connective tissue that holds the intestines in place relax, and fluid and food flow more easily. The improvement in blood circulation (30 to 40 percent of the body's total blood volume is in the abdomen) and deeper breathing that result facilitate greater oxygen supply, so the head grows clearer and concentration improves. Nutrients are better absorbed into the blood and reach more of the body. Circulation of lymph through abdominal lymph nodes, which are concentrated around the navel, also increases, enhancing the body's immunity and discharge of waste and toxins. Even the vital energy in the abdominal core is strengthened and circulated more easily and widely, enhancing overall vitality.

Seeing many people experience amazing changes of body and mind through Belly Button Healing, I began pondering how they could feel its effects more easily, which is when I created the tool called Healing Life. As shown in the image on the next page, this tool is shaped like the letter T, which allows you to hold it with both hands while pressing your navel. If you don't have a Healing Life, you can use your fingers or the end of a blunt stick or marker for Belly Button Healing.

You can do Belly Button Healing while sitting, lying down, or standing. For Pineal Gland Meditation, a sitting posture is recommended. If a half-lotus meditation posture is uncomfortable for you, sit in a chair with both feet flat on the floor.

Start by repeatedly raising and lowering your shoulders to release the tension in your shoulders and chest. Rotate your neck or move your head to the left and right, releasing the tension in your neck.

Close your eyes, take a deep breath, and exhale. Focus on your body, imagining that you're looking inside your body with your mind's eye. Try to sense how your body feels right now, so you can compare the feeling before and after doing Belly Button Healing. How mindful are you of your body, how comfortable does your chest feel, and how deeply into your lower abdomen does your breathing sink?

Now you're ready to begin Belly Button Healing. The approach is really easy. All you have to do is place a tool or your fingers on your navel and press it rhythmically and repeatedly. If you're using your fingers, bring together the index, middle, and ring fingers of both hands, to press your belly button. Do this for about three to five minutes. Let your mouth open slightly, and continuously breathe out the stagnant energy in your body.

Completing this movement doesn't mean you're done with the exercise, however. It's important to do Joshik, breath control, next. Turn your palms upward and place them on your knees, close your eyes, and straighten your back. Relax your shoulders and chest as you continue to exhale through your mouth, discharging any stagnant energy remaining in your body. Then close your mouth and breathe deeply and smoothly. Your breathing will grow gradually deeper and more comfortable.

Now, using your mind's eye, look inside your body. Continue breathing while you focus on the feelings in your abdomen. What do you feel compared to before you did this exercise?

Do you feel warmth in your abdomen or lower back? Do you feel your breath deeply sink into your lower abdomen? Do you feel your abdomen naturally expanding and contracting on its own? What about the sensations in your chest? Do you feel less emotion and more peace of mind? It's not easy to experience all these energy phenomena the first time, but everyone can feel their minds relaxing and their breath deepening and becoming more comfortable.

If you have a sense of magnetism when you do Joshik after Belly Button Healing, which often feels like a pushing and pulling sensation in your abdomen, that is the energy of the lower dahnjon. Focus on that feeling. As you continue breathing, it will be as if you are fanning the flames in a furnace, and your dahnjon will gradually fill with energy. This is Dahnjon Breathing, using energy to strengthen the dahnjon. Usually, it's difficult even for those who have trained extensively in Dahnjon Breathing to feel a strong sensation of heat and magnetism with breathing alone. But you can feel it after just three minutes of Belly Button Healing—a sensation that would take about thirty minutes of Dahnjon Breathing to experience.

Holding onto that feeling, do Joshik for a while and observe your dahnjon with your mind's eye. Calm will come over your mind, and you'll enter a state of Jigam, which is when your emotions have stopped and you experience a pure, unadulterated mind. During this practice, the dahnjon acts as an anchor, keeping your mind fully in your body and preventing your attention from going outside. By anchoring your mind in your dahnjon while breathing deeply, you'll enter a state of Geumchok, focusing entirely within. Once you've attained the states of Jigam, Joshik, and Geumchok, you're ready to experience the next step of Pineal Gland Meditation.

Keeping the Mind in the Dahnjon

I'll give you one last important tip for connecting with your body continuously in your daily life, without doing any movement at all. In Sundo this is called "keeping the mind in the dahnjon." You can feel right away how incredible its effects are.

First, focus your mind on some object in front of you, and try to feel your body as you do so. Do you really sense the feeling of your body, including your breathing? It's not easy, right?

Now try focusing your mind on your dahnjon in your lower abdomen. You'll feel it more if you close your eyes, but it's definitely possible even with your eyes open. With your mind in your dahnjon, try to feel your breathing. You'll be able to sense your breathing becoming more comfortable, gradually going deeper, all the way to your lower abdomen. The deeper your breathing, the more energy is accumulating in your dahnjon. Gradually your dahnjon will grow warm, as if your breath is working a bellows, heating a furnace there. This is a shortcut to connecting with your body and to Jungchoong, charging yourself with jung energy.

You can focus on your dahnjon at any time in your daily life. Better yet, you can do it constantly throughout the day! You can do it when you're working at your computer, when you're cooking, when you're walking or in a car, even when you're talking with people. Try to always keep part of your attention in your dahnjon and not let it be entirely captured by the jostling confusion outside. Anchor your mind in your core.

Have you ever played with a roly-poly toy? No matter how hard you push it, the doll pops back up, returning to its original position. The secret is that the toy's center of gravity is situated firmly at the bottom. Our dahnjon plays that same role. If you keep your mind in your dahnjon, then no matter how many negative thoughts or emotions fill your head, no matter how many waves of external information wash over you, you'll be able to retain your center without being knocked down or swept away.

Try to practice connecting with your body regularly through the various methods that have been introduced in this chapter. Even better, incorporate the training into your daily life. For example, do Toe Tapping before going to sleep at night and do Belly Button Healing when you need refreshing in the afternoon.

It's crucial to make a habit of connecting with your body, especially before going to sleep. Do some stretching and then Toe Tapping as you get ready to sleep. Take time to release the energy of fatigue built up during the day—the energy of your complicated thoughts and feelings. Collect your attention, scattered outward by your various activities, and focus it completely within. Sleep is a time for connecting with your unconsciousness, and for recharging your energy. The time of quiet relaxation before going to sleep is the best time for connecting with yourself. You'll feel a big difference in the quality of your sleep and your condition the next day when you fall asleep after first cleansing your energy and connecting with yourself.

If you make a habit of connecting with yourself, it will become a kind of ritual, a happy time—even the most important time of your day. The fact that you have a body, a refuge to which you can always return for rest from the suffering of life, should be an incredible comfort and consolation. Be grateful for your body since it is the place you can find true rest. Your precious life is living and breathing, here and now. You can always care for it and love yourself, without relying on others. Take the time at least once a day to set aside all your thoughts and emotions and connect completely with your body. This small difference affects your happiness and quality of life greatly.

CHAPTER 7

Connecting with Your Soul

The reason we practice keeping our mind in the body, as explained in the previous chapter, is to encounter the soul. Our souls are in our bodies, existing in our hearts as energy. That's why the heart is called the "Human Palace." It is the place containing the identity of one person—the being called "you." Connecting with your soul is the second step of Pineal Gland Meditation.

Unfortunately, the energy we carry in our hearts is not only that of the soul. If our hearts contained only the energy of our pure souls, the energy of love and compassion, why would we ever worry or be anxious about anything? We would be full of love, joy, and happiness every moment. But our hearts contain a complex mixture of subtle energies. Along with the energy of the soul are the energies of negative emotions such as jealousy, envy, anger, anxiety, inferiority or superiority feelings, shame, and guilt. The energy of the soul and the energy of emotion are in a tug-of-war, playing a power game with each other. Seesawing back and forth, the power of emotion decreases when the power of the soul increases, and the power of the soul rises when the power of emotion falls.

How does one develop the power of the soul energy to connect with the soul? First, we separate our soul energy from the energy of our emotions. Otherwise, we'll be confused about where to focus, not knowing whether our emotions are our soul or our soul is our emotions. Only when our emotions calm down and become quiet will we be able to detect the energy of our soul.

The way to separate soul energy from emotional energy is the practice of Jigam—stopping emotion. In Sundo, "Jigam training" or "energy sensitizing" is training for actually feeling energy. You are probably aware that our bodies are electromagnetic energy fields, but do you feel and use the energy in your body? The key practice I consistently teach wherever I go is Jigam. Why is that so crucial? Feeling energy through Jigam leads to feeling your soul, since the energy in your heart is the energy of your soul. To feel energy, you connect with yourself by focusing inward. Also called "energy meditation," Jigam is a step toward entering the unseen world, the world of energy.

The greatest impediments to meditation are thoughts wandering through the mind. Meditators try various methods to rid themselves of those thoughts. Some meditate while staring at a point drawn on a wall or at a flickering candle flame, some continuously focus on a koan, some repeat a mantra or specific phrase, and some concentrate entirely on the breath coming and going from their bodies.

Such methods generally make use of breathing and concentrating one's mind. Energy meditation adds one more element: feeling energy. If you just sit there with your eyes closed, distracting thoughts will arise in your mind as you revert to your thinking brain. But if you focus your awareness on the feeling of energy and keep focusing on expanding that feeling, your tangled thoughts will fall away before you know it. You will be fully immersed in yourself. When your thoughts and emotions quiet down, you will enter a true meditative state.

In this state, when you do energy meditation, your brain waves also calm down. They usually follow a beta pattern in your daily life, but when you are very relaxed, they assume an alpha pattern, which has a lower frequency. When you first enter Jigam, your brain waves are in an alpha pattern. As you go deeper and deeper into the Jigam state, they further slow down and stabilize as theta waves, which is a state between waking and sleeping. When theta brain waves predominate, you are easily able to enter your deep internal consciousness, where you can then access expanded insight, creative thinking, and problem-solving ability.

Jigam practice begins with our hands since they are very sensitive and are designed to send finely tuned messages using the sense of touch to our brains. On the Penfield diagram, which maps out sensory information from different parts of the body to areas of the brain, the hands are depicted as the largest part since a higher percentage of the brain is devoted to processing their input. In other words, our brains are exquisitely sensitive to the sensations we feel in our hands. That's why during Jigam training, you first concentrate on the feeling of energy on your palms. Even beginners often have a very good energy sensation this way. Those whose training has progressed are able to gradually expand that feeling to their arms and chest, and throughout their body. Your arms may even begin to move very slowly with the energy in a kind of dance.

Once your whole body is sensitized to energy, the sense of your body as a solid form will disappear. Instead, you will feel more fluid and a state of light energy. I call this the "energy body." Although your physical body is still there, now it feels more like transparent energy than a solid mass.

Experiencing your energy body is an essential part of Pineal Gland Meditation, for this is a process of transformation, of expanding your awareness from just a physical body to include an energy body—and, going further, to develop your spiritual body. In this chapter, I will explain how you can develop awareness of your energy body, and in the following chapter I'll talk about the spiritual body.

To experience your energy body, the soul energy in your heart needs to be activated. No matter how much physical training you do, it doesn't guarantee that you experience transformational energy phenomena from physical body to energy body. Jigam training is the best way to begin. It may be difficult to experience everything in just one try, so you'll want to practice this repeatedly.

Jigam: Feeling Energy

First, relax your body as much as you can. Standing, do gentle stretching; rotate or stretch your neck, too. Shrug your shoulders repeatedly up and down to relax your shoulders and chest.

Slowly sit down in a chair or on the floor in a meditation posture. Straighten your lower back and place your hands on your knees. Close your eyes and steady your breathing. When your breathing is calm and stable, tap your fingertips together about 50 times. Then, rub your palms rapidly together for about 10 to 20 seconds. Afterward, hold your hands about an inch apart, palms facing.

Gently close your eyes and focus on the feelings in your hands. To keep your mind there, think to yourself, "Hands . . . hands . . . hands." What feelings do you get? You may feel heat on your palms, a tingling in your fingertips, an itching or crawling sensation between your fingers. That is the feeling of energy.

Now spread your palms a little farther apart, breathing in, and then bring them close together again, breathing out. Repeat

this motion, immersing yourself in the feelings in your hands as you very slowly move them apart and then bring them closer together, expanding and contracting the space between them.

If your sense is acute, the feelings of heat and magnetism in your hands will be amplified. You may feel as if there is a rubber balloon full of air between your hands, alternately expanding and contracting, pushing and pulling. Moving your hands so that they are slightly off center from each other, try shifting that imaginary balloon around. Thinking of it as a ball of energy, roll it between your hands this way and that, very slowly. Imagining this energy ball gradually growing larger and stronger, focus on the feelings between your hands.

Do you get a feeling of energy between your hands? If you do, isn't it amazing? That is your energy. Through your mind's ability to focus, your body's electromagnetic bioenergy field is amplified and its energy grows stronger. Like a young child playing with a balloon, let yourself really enjoy the feelings of that mysterious energy as you roll the energy ball between your hands.

With time, you will become completely focused on the feeling of energy. No negative feelings can interrupt the sense of becoming immersed in the world of pure energy.

Feeling Soul Energy in the Heart

For the next stage of energy training, close your eyes and slowly bring the palms of your hands in front of your chest. Leave about two inches between your palms and your chest. Imagine the energy you just felt now being emitted from your palms and flowing into your chest. Where the mind focuses, energy is bound to follow. "Chest . . . chest . . . chest . . ." focus your mind in your chest, which holds the energy of your soul and your emotions. Concentrate on trying to feel your chest as you breathe.

What sensations do you detect? Does your chest feel blocked and stuffy? Or do you have a comfortable, open feeling? The more you feel that your chest is blocked, the more your emotional energy is predominating and the energy of your soul is contracting. Try to detect the state of your soul energy right now—and keep sending warm, pure energy from your palms to your soul. Imagine it healing your heart. Concentrate your mind on your chest, repeating to yourself, "My soul . . . my soul . . . my soul."

Are you being connected with the soul energy in your heart? If you get that feeling of connection, say this to your soul: "I love you. I love you, my soul." And, with the utmost sincerity, offer an apology to your soul: "I'm sorry, my soul. I didn't know you were always there. I was disconnected from you. I'm really sorry."

As you say this, you may feel the stress and trauma you have been carrying with you move in your chest. It may feel hot or cold or as if pressure is being lifted from your chest. You may even shed tears as your soul begins to be freed from its cage of emotion. Relax and exhale through your mouth strongly at this time to release this old, stagnant energy.

As you do this, say, "I love you" and "I'm sorry" to your soul with sincerity, so that your soul can hear it. The withdrawn, hidden parts of your soul will begin to awaken. The moment you connect with your soul, you'll have the feeling that the energy of your soul is moving. Continue telling your soul the things you've been wanting to say. You'll feel the soul's energy gradually reviving.

Having been suppressed by emotion, your soul will be relieved and will now revive. Feel soul energy fully filling your chest. Do you feel it? Keep focusing on that feeling. That is your soul.

Your soul recovers its original position as the master of your being the instant you restore your broken connection with it. The soul is your true self. If your emotions have been acting as master, let your soul now recover its rightful place. Continue sending energy into your chest, imagining that your soul energy is spreading to your whole body.

Now slowly move the palms of your hands over your body's energy field, from top to bottom. As you do so, send energy to your head, arms, trunk, and legs, surrounding your body in a capsule of energy. Think of a ray of energy, like a beam of light, coming out of your hands, healing every cell of your body. Try to feel the energy of each part of your body being activated.

Finally, bring your palms back in front of your chest, sending energy to your soul. Visualize the bright, golden soul energy in your heart spreading out to your face, arms, legs—your whole body. Your body is gradually being transformed into an energy body. It will feel progressively lighter, brighter, and more transparent, as if your physical body has disappeared. That is the feeling of the energy body. Slowly lower your hands onto your knees, take a deep breath, and exhale as you open your eyes.

What did you feel through this energy meditation? Was the feeling gentle, soft, and peaceful? That is the feeling of your soul. If you have trouble finding this feeling the first time, do not worry. Keep trying to connect with your soul and you will soon feel it. Some days it may be more difficult than others, but your soul will answer your sincerity in the end.

Your soul received your body and was born into this world years ago. When you were very young, the feeling of your soul was still there, a living thing. As a small child, you laughed innocently, everything in the world seeming beautiful. As you grew into adulthood, though, your head filled with information ally declined and may even have eventually broken. Then, the energy of your soul contracted, and the emotional energy in your heart grew to fill the available space until you became a person led about by the voice of your emotions. Now, you sometimes suppress even those feelings, acting as directed by the thoughts in your head—ideas given to you by a world saying that you must do this and you must do that. And, sometimes, the needs and desires of your body are beyond the control of the rational thoughts in your head.

The human is a complex being. In the heart are the soul and the emotions, which is confusing enough, but added to the mix are the thoughts of the head and the desires of the body, causing great chaos. If you are well connected with your soul, however, you can get back up when life knocks you over and regain your balance. But, if thoughts, emotions, and desires take the soul's place, you end up bewildered. The emotions in your heart tell you to do one thing, the thoughts in your head tell you to do something else, and your body wants to move in a completely different direction. Your head (thoughts), heart (emotions), and body (desires) all move in different directions.

In such confusion, what do you base your decisions on? Do you do what your thoughts want? Do you do as the emotions in your heart want, or as the desires of your body want? The surest way to avoid regret is to choose what your soul, your true self, wants. If you choose what your thoughts, emotions, or desires want, sooner or later you may regret that choice. To follow the voice of your soul, though, you have to know what your soul really wants. That's why connecting with your soul is essential. Your soul is the clear, pure energy you just felt while doing Jigam training, an energy of 100 percent purity. It's pure love and compassion, free of attachments and conditions, an energy warm and bright like sunshine.

The energy of the soul is the energy of a great love, a love that you can use to heal yourself, others, and the world. Growing your soul means continuously developing your soul's energy, enabling that energy of great love to come from your heart. But when you've just connected with your soul, it's like a pure but vulnerable infant and may be overwhelmed by massive waves of emotion again at any time. You need to care for your just-awakened soul, just as you would care for a newborn baby. Continuously cleansing the energy of your emotions is essential for this—and here we find the secret to passing the Soul Gate, the second gate in Sundo.

The energy of the soul in our heart wants to grow and ultimately reach the Heavenly Palace in our brain. The gate we have to pass first is the Soul Gate, located in the neck. Touch your neck with your hand. The neck acts as a bridge connecting your chest and head, and this gate has a secret: like a filtering device, it keeps unpurified energy from rising to the brain. Imagine what would happen if the energy of negative emotions roiling in your heart, like sadness and anger, were to rise straight into your brain. Filled with the energy of sadness or anger, your brain would be unable to perform its proper functions. Fortunately, the Soul Gate filters emotional energy, keeping it from rising haphazardly into the brain.

Interpreted through the lens of modern medicine, the Soul Gate is similar in function to the thyroid gland. When it functions normally, you are fine, but when your thyroid gland develops problems, you experience an emotional regulation disorder. You're often irritable, saying things you later regret and failing to regulate your mood. People under a great deal of stress, who suppress their emotional energy in their chests, are especially prone to thyroid problems because the emotional energy in their chests—fire energy—rises to their necks and continuously attacks the thyroid.

If the soul energy in your heart is to rise to the Heavenly Palace, it must first pass the filter of the Soul Gate. What should you do to make that possible? Only energy in a pure, mature, and light state can pass the filter of the Soul Gate. Our soul energy isn't pure and mature when it is caught by the heavy, cloudy energy of the emotions in our hearts. When we purify the emotional energy that holds onto our souls, they are set free and are able to rise. I'll teach you a few methods for doing this.

5 Healing Words Meditation

The first method is 5 Healing Words Meditation. While you meditate, say, "I'm sorry," "Forgive me" (or, "I will forgive you"), "Thank you," "I love you," or "Help me," releasing the emotional energy long accumulating in your heart. This is for releasing resentment. You can bring some object, situation, or person to mind as you meditate, but first you need to release the resentment you have toward yourself. Only then can you connect with yourself as deep emotional cleansing takes place within you.

Although it's probably true for all forms of meditation, for 5 Healing Words Meditation in particular, you need to enter into your deep, internal consciousness. A true release of resentment doesn't happen on the level of superficial external consciousness, on the level of thinking. When you enter deeply into your internal consciousness, you discover bundles of emotion that have formed inside you. Do that for a while, and those bundles of emotion, recognized or unrecognized, will rise to the surface of consciousness. The most effective method for entering internal consciousness is to be carried on energy. This is the method of Jigam training described earlier in this chapter.

After feeling energy in your hands with Jigam, described on pages 96–97, continue with the following training.

Close your eyes, and once your hands are sufficiently sensitized to energy, bring your palms in front of your chest. Continue sending to energy from your palms to your soul. Try to feel the state of your soul. Is it lonely? Is it sad? Is it suffering, or frustrated? You, and no one else, have left your soul in that state for so long. When that realization washes over you, you will feel sorry for your soul.

Tell your soul, "Oh, my soul, I'm truly sorry for leaving you like this. Immersed in other people or things, I failed to really take interest in you. I'm truly sorry for troubling you, for making you lonely. Please forgive me."

Feel sorry for failing to love yourself, possibly even hating and disparaging yourself, calling yourself stupid, ugly, or incompetent. Sincerely apologize for being the one who has crushed your soul's confidence. Bringing to mind how you have been treating yourself, convey to your soul all the regret you're feeling. On hearing those words, your soul's energy will awaken and move. You may even weep hot tears of remorse. Those tears signal a release of resentments, forgiveness from your soul. You can truly connect with your soul at last when you ask yourself for forgiveness.

Embrace yourself with both of your arms, giving yourself a strong hug. And tell yourself, "I love you so much. I'll never make you lonely again." And express your gratitude and resolve to your soul, "Thank you for watching over me even though I haven't acknowledged you, even though I've troubled you. Now I'll protect you. Help me live for your growth. Help me always to treasure this feeling of you."

You can use this same approach to release resentments in your relationships with others. If you feel resentment or guilt toward someone, those emotions act as stumbling blocks inhibiting the growth of your soul. You can't help but feel continuous discomfort in one corner of your heart if you feel guilty about past actions and feel indebted to someone else. Only when you have no such feelings can your soul be truly free, your heart genuinely at peace. Don't you want to feel that freedom and peace? Forgiveness requires courage. Being able to understand and forgive someone means that your mind and heart are large enough for that. You can embrace others to the extent that your heart allows. Use the following exercise to rid yourself of deep-seated anger from old hurts.

To do meditation for releasing resentment against others, first do the Jigam training that was described previously. Enter your internal consciousness, and when you are focused on yourself, place your hands on your knees, palms up.

Now, close your eyes and bring to mind the face of someone you resent or have been unable to forgive. Try to feel in your heart the emotional energy directed toward that person. What kind of emotion is it? You might hate the other person for some harm they have caused you, or you might resent them for not meeting your expectations. The love you once had has changed into resentment, which means you are attached and clinging to those emotions. Does resenting the other person free your mind and bring you peace? Isn't it causing pain in your heart? Resentment is the energy of a massive attachment hindering your freedom. Isn't it time to let it go? Try to make up your mind now to forgive and free yourself from those negative feelings—not for the other person's sake, but for your own.

Turning your palms toward your chest, send healing energy into your heart. Use that energy to caress and comfort your heart, which has been troubled by the other person. You can heal and comfort yourself in this way. To completely heal your heart, let go of that tangle of attachments, the resentments you've been clinging to. Once again bring the person's face to mind. Say: "I've been really troubled because of you, so I've resented you. I've realized, though, that resentment is also an attachment. I now want to let go of that resentment and be free. So I forgive you. My heart wants to find peace now. I'm sorry for resenting you."

After voicing your forgiveness in this way, take a deep breath, then slowly exhale, "Hoo . . ." You'll probably feel much greater comfort in your heart. Patting yourself on the chest, praise yourself for having the great courage to forgive, telling yourself, "Yeah, you did well!"

If there's someone from whom you want to seek forgiveness, use this meditation. The more you repeat it, the deeper a connection with yourself and others you will feel.

Letting Go Meditation

The second method for cleansing emotional energy and freeing the soul is Letting Go Meditation. Excessive attachments to external things—such as money, objects, and reputation, as well as people—block the growth of our souls. Whether you like or dislike someone or something, if it's excessive and hinders your connection to your true self, then it's an attachment. I don't mean to suggest that you shouldn't take any interest in these things at all. If you can make good use of them, they can contribute to the growth of your soul. But this requires that you see them as things that contribute to the growth of your soul rather than as possessions or attachments. To do that, more than anything else, you must be centered solidly in your soul and be able to let your attachments go.

Let me introduce you to Letting Go Meditation for discarding attachments and becoming a free soul.

First, relax your body, and sit down in a chair or on the floor in a meditation posture. Straighten your lower back and place your hands on your knees. Close your eyes and steady your breathing.

Slowly bring one hand in front of your chest, with your palm cupped as if to receive falling water. Imagine your hand as the cup of your soul. Once there was nothing in the cup of your soul, but as you've lived your life, many things have filled it, gradually weighing down your soul.

Bring to mind all of the attachments and negative emotions that you have in the cup of your soul. It is now time to let them go. This requires courage, and only you can make that choice.

Ready? Count to three in your mind and slowly turn your palm down, pouring out the things in the cup of your soul. Completely let go of everything that burdened and troubled your soul. Feel an ardent desire to become a free soul, soaring freely in the sky, like a bird.

Now spread your arms out to your sides and flap them up and down like wings. Fly freely into the wide open sky. Your energy gradually grows lighter and brighter as you soar through the heavens.

Then, slowly bring your hands down, laying them on your knees with your palms up. Look inside yourself. What are you feeling in your heart right now?

Give thanks to everything you have experienced in your life, both good and bad, bitter and sweet, for it has been meaningful and has taught you. Let peace from this knowledge begin to spread in your heart. The seed of your soul starts to grow when your heart is at peace.

Healing Sound Meditation Level 1

Another method for cleansing your emotions and freeing your soul is Healing Sound Meditation, which makes use of the vibrations of your own voice for meditation and healing. Have you ever been moved to tears by a song? This happens because the vibrations and emotions of music can resonate with your heart, which is why music has such amazing cathartic appeal. The majority of spiritual traditions, both Eastern and Western, have meditative methods that make use of the voice. In Christian traditions, for example, the word "Amen" is used, and Asian traditions commonly use the mantra "Om."

Whatever kind of voice you may have, you can use it to cleanse your emotions and free your soul. Healing Sound Meditation starts with singing a song in your mind. Try simply using the sound "ah." The main thing is that it shouldn't be a song you already know. Sing an impromptu song and create the melody as you go along, a song without any set intervals or beat.

First close your eyes, concentrating on your heart, and make the sound "ah," long and slow, several times. Next add a melody. There are no rules—just do whatever you want, go with whatever comes out of you. Using your voice, try to express the feelings in your heart. Sing a song that no one else can imitate. Create rhythms and waves that are uniquely your own, a song made in an unrepeatable instant of improvised composition. It's not difficult at all! Let it come out naturally—like breathing, like walking, like speaking.

"I feel at peace while listening to this sound"—having this feeling is enough. Our brains have an amazing sense for balance and harmony. Keep at it, and your brain will make harmonious sounds, adjusting pitch, stress, and rhythm. It will create a sound that's good listening for your brain, a sound that brings peace and fullness to your heart. When you are used to singing with the sound "ah," try using other vowels like "oh" and "oo," changing the vowels as you sing, not sticking to a single sound. The vibrations coming from your voice will open your heart.

Healing Sound Meditation Level 2

Now I want to introduce a method of Healing Sound Meditation I've named *Jitalk*. *Ji* in Korean means "Earth," and Jitalk refers to the voice of all earth citizens, not to any specific language currently spoken. This is a song that attaches a melody to syllables that aren't words as we normally use them.

Think of it as gibberish, like a baby trying to talk. It's singing a song using whatever syllables come out of your mouth, like, "Ama yone, nepeuta koneme." You're composing lyrics and music, even singing a song in an impromptu way. You have to do it without any thought or hesitation, without anticipating what syllables or melodies may come out of your mouth. How creative is that? Creating and singing without any time to think is a shocking idea, isn't it? We are used to judging ourselves and stopping our own creative expression, but this is your chance to be free. Singing properly and musical talent is beside the point. As you allow this to happen, your brain becomes more flexible and creative since you're using it in a different way than usual.

With conventional songs, you may worry about whether you're getting the lyrics or melody right and how others will evaluate you, activating the thinking brain. There's no need for that with Jitalk. You compose lyrics and music on the fly, so no one can judge you for not getting it right! You simply enter your deep internal consciousness and express the feelings in your heart as they are.

In the flow of Pineal Gland Meditation, Jitalk can purify

emotional energy in your chest and help the soul's energy pass through the Soul Gate. After ordinary singing, we typically experience the chest and throat opening. Similarly, after Jitalk, the stagnant energy in the chest and throat is released. The difference is that you can focus better on the feeling of the soul when you do Jitalk.

Practice Jitalk after connecting with your soul through Jigam training or meditation. Of course, it's fine to do Jitalk without any prior preparation, when you're alone and you want to connect with your soul and express the feeling of it.

Now try following along with this Jitalk meditation:

First close your eyes and do Jigam, feeling the energy between your hands. Turning your palms toward your chest, connect with the energy of your soul and try to feel what your soul wants. Our souls want to be free. They want to be loved and feel greater light and peace. Express in song the desires of your soul, its longing to rise toward the light of divinity in your brain. The more sincere you are, the better your soul energy will be expressed through your voice. Any syllable is fine—just put into song whatever sound spontaneously comes out of you. You don't need to make it loud, either; start with a quiet voice. It may feel awkward at first, but try immersing yourself in the feelings in your heart. Getting it right or wrong, doing it well or poorly—there are no such standards. It's enough to simply express the feelings in your heart. Do that for a while and your brain will become more versatile, the energy of your soul reviving.

Doing Jitalk will gradually feel more natural, and eventually you'll feel your rhythm slowing and your breathing becoming deeper. The sound will come not only from your throat but from your heart and even from deep within your lower abdomen, resonating in your heart and brain. The vibrations of the sound will reverberate, spreading to the roof of your mouth, your nose, eyes, the inside of your ears, and deep within your brain. Imagine your voice making your skin and bones vibrate, penetrating every cell in your body, healing them. You may even discover a beautiful, sacred sound coming from within you, seeming to echo through the heavens.

While doing Jitalk, you can move your hands in front of your chest, freely and slowly, going with the energy and using your hands to express the feeling of your soul, like you are doing an energy dance. Really opening your heart and brain, try to express what your soul truly wants— its desire to be completely free and light, its longing for a world filled with light and love. If you continue this, the energy of your soul will pass the Soul Gate, rising to the Heavenly Palace in your brain. As you hold onto that feeling after doing Jitalk, it's best to immediately follow it with the meditation for connecting with your divinity described in the following chapter.

Aroma Energy Meditation

One more tool you can use for purifying your emotions and freeing your soul is aromatherapy oil. Essential oils containing ingredients such as lavender, peppermint, sage, eucalyptus, and rosemary are generally considered good for the brain and effective for meditation. The oil I want to introduce is an essential oil named Bird of the Soul, created by mixing 17 different aromas. The name symbolizes the energy of the soul in our hearts, rising and flying free like a bird. Bird of the Soul oil helps activate all seven chakras in our bodies, particularly the heart and third-eye chakras, the middle and upper dahnjons.

Here is how to use Bird of the Soul oil, or any of the other oils I mentioned above, when doing Pineal Gland Meditation:

After doing Pineal Gland Meditation Step 1 (connecting with your body) and while doing Step 2 (connecting with your soul), apply some of the oil to the tip of your nose, to your third-eye chakra between your eyebrows, and on the inside of your wrists. Bring your wrists to your nose, deeply inhaling and smelling the aroma for about 30 seconds. The aroma will refresh your brain. Imagine that the aroma is spreading to your whole body, seeping into all the cells and transforming it into an energy body.

Very, very slowly, move your hands apart to the sides of your body as you visualize your body transforming into an energy body from your head to your chest, belly, arms, and legs. Now move your hands freely and slowly, doing an energy dance, activating your energy body for awhile. Then, place your hands on your knees and breathe deeply, further activating and expanding your energy field.

When you have the feeling that your physical body is transforming into an energy body, you're ready for the final step of Pineal Gland Meditation: connecting with your divinity.

CHAPTER 8

Connecting with Your Divinity

Having passed the Soul Gate, the energy of the soul now rises to the Heavenly Palace in the final step of Pineal Gland Meditation. This is the energy center called the upper dahnjon, centered on the brainstem and pineal gland in the deepest part of the brain.

The pineal is a pinecone-shaped endocrine gland located behind and slightly below the center of the brain. It is immediately behind the top part of the brainstem, which handles major vital functions such as breathing, respiration, and blood pressure. While most of the brain's organs form symmetric pairs, one in the left and one in the right hemisphere, the pineal gland exists alone in the deepest part of the brain.

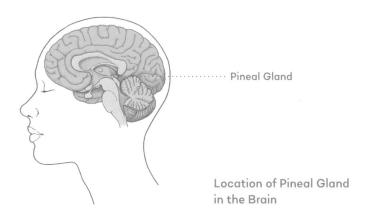

················· Pineal Gland

Location of Pineal Gland
in the Brain

The pineal gland appears early in fetal development and is about five to eight millimeters long—less than a third of an inch. Reddish gray in color, it weighs about 0.1 to 0.18 grams. This gland is well developed in lower animals, with a structure like that of an eye; in higher animals, the function of the pineal gland is said to have been reduced to that of an "atrophied eye."

The pineal gland grows until a child reaches the age of one or two; it begins to calcify in puberty, when calcium, magnesium, phosphorus, and other elements begin building up on the gland. Calcified structures can be seen on the pineal gland using X-ray and other imaging techniques. Scientists call these "brain sand." If calcification is severe, these structures may become hard, like teeth or bones. Calcification of the pineal gland is reportedly associated with Alzheimer's and other brain diseases.

The pineal gland is closely associated with light; it detects light entering through the scalp, secreting the hormone melatonin to regulate sleep time and reproductive periods. Melatonin secretion increases at night, making us naturally sleepy, and decreases with exposure to light in the morning, opening our eyes. Melatonin not only promotes sleep but is also a powerful antioxidant, reportedly having a significant impact on aging and immunity.

Many cultures and traditions around the world directly or symbolically emphasize the importance of the pineal gland. The Eye of Horus, considered a symbol of absolute power, health, and knowledge, is frequently found on ancient Egyptian artifacts, and the Ajna or third-eye chakra is known as a center of intuition and insight in the Hindu traditions of India. Both of these are associated with the pineal gland. Most images of the Buddha show a protruding point or glass jewel between the eyebrows. According to Buddhist scriptures, light pouring out from a place in the Buddha's forehead illuminates the world.

In Eastern Taoism, most immortals are shown meditating in a lotus posture beneath a tree from which a pinecone is hanging. What's more, there is a massive bronze statue of a pinecone at the entrance to the Vatican, and the pinecone shape appears on the staff used by the pope when celebrating the Mass. In diverse traditions, the pineal gland has symbolized wisdom, an exalted spirit, and ultimate knowledge able to pierce the veil of illusion in the world.

Clockwise from left: The Eye of Horus, a symbol that was found on ancient Egyptian artifacts; Ajna chakra in the Hindu traditions; a statue of a pine cone at the entrance to the Vatican; a point between the eyebrows of a sculpture of Buddha

Throughout the ages, people have sought the elixir of life that will bring them enlightenment and the blessings of heaven. The philosopher's stone, the nectar of the gods, and the fountain of youth—these are symbols of this constant yearning found in the long-developed traditions of both East and West.

When talking about Pineal Gland Meditation, this elixir may be the DMT (dimethyltryptamine) the pineal gland secretes, a substance that gives rise to deep spiritual experiences. If your pineal gland is activated, when you meditate you may get the feeling that a thick, sticky liquid or something like honey is being secreted by your brain and coming down along your spine. It feels as if oil is flowing along your endocrine and nervous systems, entering every organ in your body. A body and brain that once felt stiff and depleted now seem remarkably fluid and flexible, giving you the feeling that you've recovered the energy of youth. When the Bible refers to the Holy Spirit and holy anointing oil, it may be in reference to such energy phenomena. Likewise, Greek myths speak of ambrosia as the food and drink of the gods, and in Hinduism *ojas* means the fluid of life.

Besides the feeling of fluid, when the energy of your pineal gland is activated, you are able to experience the ecstasy of light shining before your eyes—even when your eyes are closed, even in great darkness. This light is said to be the third eye opening. In Sundo, this phenomenon is called Shinmyung, which means that the shin energy in your upper dahnjon is shining bright.

To activate your pineal gland, it's important to develop the entire energy system of the upper dahnjon surrounding it. More energy points are concentrated in the head and face than any-where else in our body, and these include several major points that must be activated to develop the upper dahnjon. The first is the *Indang* point, centered between the eyebrows. As shown in the image below, if you go up from the Indang you'll find the

Junjung point and the *Baekhwe*, which is in the crown of the head. Go from the crown of your head toward the back, following the centerline of your head, and you'll come to the *Noeho* point at the very back, where the skull protrudes the most. A couple of inches down from there is the *Ahmun* point, in the indentation where the neck meets the head. Finally, the *Taeyang* points are located at the temples.

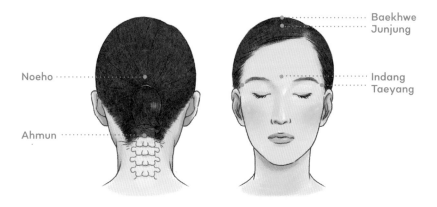

Baekhwe
Junjung
Noeho
Indang
Taeyang
Ahmun

Important Energy Points on the Head

These energy points are situated in symmetrical pairs with the pineal gland in the middle—the Indang with the Noeho, the Junjung with the Ahmun, and the two Taeyang points on each side of the head. In the process of developing your upper dahnjon, not only will you feel each energy point being activated, but you will also sense the energy pathways from each energy point being connected to the pineal gland. When these energy channels all open up so that the energy system of the upper dahnjon is activated, so is the pineal gland at its center.

There are different methods for activating the upper dahnjon system, but the two presented here are especially effective and easy to follow.

Activating Brain Energy with Hands

Brain Jigam, the first method for upper dahnjon activation, is a form of brain energy meditation. With ordinary Jigam training, described in Chapter 7, you can feel energy between your hands. In Brain Jigam training, you bring your hands up around your head to feel the energy between your brain and your hands. You can't physically touch the brain with your hands, but through Brain Jigam training you can stimulate it using energy.

Sitting in a meditation posture with your eyes closed, first do Jigam training to activate the energy between your hands. Once the energy field between your hands is sufficiently activated, slowly bring your hands along the sides of your head. Leave a gap of about two to three inches between your hands and your head. Imagine a bright, powerful energy being emitted by your hands and entering your brain.

Now move your hands slightly farther out from your head and then bring them close again; repeat this movement. You're doing Jigam training between your hands and brain, like you did Jigam between your hands. Do this for a while and you'll experience a magnetic feeling, as if something is pushing and pulling between your hands and brain. A magnetic energy field is being activated around your brain.

Once you really feel the energy between your hands and brain, bring your palms in front of your face to send energy into it. Smile, feeling your facial muscles relaxing. Slowly move your hands in front of your face from top to bottom without touching it, as if washing your face with energy, sending bright healing energy to every part of it. The face is directly connected to the brain, so opening the energy points in the face is necessary for activating the brain's energy.

Now very slowly raise your hands, going from forehead to crown along the centerline of your head, sending energy into your brain. From the crown, lower your hands slowly backward along the centerline of your head. Now move your hands freely around your head to send energy into every nook and cranny of your brain. If parts feel a little blocked, spend more time on those places, ensuring that energy can flow throughout your brain. Imagine putting on a helmet made of energy. As your brain gradually grows brighter and more comfortable, you will feel the expression on your face becoming more comfortable and cheerful.

So far you've sensitized your whole brain to energy. Now we'll do a meditation to activate the major energy points of your brain in a concentrated way and connect energy channels to your pineal gland. At the tip of each of your fingers is an energy point. When you send out energy through these points, it may feel as if energy light rays are coming out of your fingertips.

Begin with the Indang point. As shown in the image above, bring the back of the four fingers on both hands close to each other, keeping a little space between them and each finger as well. Close your eyes and hold your fingertips over your Indang energy point. Let energy flow naturally from your fingertips to your Indang, imagining laser energy beam being emitted. Picture the energy beam opening your Indang, going all the way to your pineal gland at the center of your brain. You may experience pressure, a pulse, or something seeming to move in your Indang point. These are phenomena that occur when the energy of a point is activated. After opening this point, keep sending an energy beam to open the channel from your Indang to your pineal gland.

Using the same method as described above, open your energy points along the centerline of your head, going from the Junjung to the Baekhwe, Noeho, Ahmun, and Taeyang. If you again open your Indang point now, you will be able to experience feelings and energy phenomena more powerfully than you did on your first try.

After you've opened all these energy points, with your hands on your knees and your eyes closed, try to detect the feelings in your brain. Do you have the sense that energy has been activated throughout the brain, making it feel lighter and brighter? Are your facial muscles more relaxed, a gentle smile on your face? If so, that's because the shin energy in your upper dahnjon has been illuminated. If you do this brain energy meditation every day, not only will your brain energy system be activated, but it will help you have a positive awareness and a cheerful expression.

Activating Brain Energy with the LifeParticle Card

LifeParticle Card Meditation is the second method for activating the brain energy system. Very simple but very powerful, this form of brain energy meditation uses a tool called the LifeParticle Card. To understand this, you first need to know what LifeParticles are and what the LifeParticle Card is.

LifeParticles are particles of life energy that you can experience when you are in a state of pure consciousness. Using a physics concept, you could say that LifeParticles are elementary particles—the smallest units of matter and energy, making up everything in the universe. The concept of LifeParticles adds the idea of consciousness to matter and energy by acknowledging the power of the mind to actually move these particles.

LifeParticles is a term I coined to express the world I experienced when I entered a state of pure consciousness through 21 days of extreme training. What I saw in that state was waves of energy moving and vibrating rapidly, filling a hologram-like space that spread out infinitely in all directions. The self I perceived then was not my physical self, but waves of light filling the cosmos—cosmic energy and cosmic mind, one with everything in the universe.

When you look at the world at this level, you come to realize that everything is made up of LifeParticles. I am LifeParticles and you are LifeParticles, as is everyone you love and everyone you hate. Flowers are LifeParticles, trees are LifeParticles; the earth, the sky, and the whole universe are all vibrating LifeParticles. Everything is interconnected and one, so you can't separate, discriminate, or hate. Dichotomous boundaries disappear. Self and other, subject and object, reality and unreality—all are part of a unified field of vibrating elementary particles.

LifeParticle Sun Image

The LifeParticle Card is what I created while thinking about how I could enable people to understand and experience LifeParticles. The image on the card is what I call the LifeParticle Sun— the source from which LifeParticles emit. This image captures the phenomena of light seen in Pineal Gland Meditation.

In diverse cultures and spiritual traditions, people have long created structures or symbols based on the principle that certain wavelengths of energy come from specific forms and colors. Hindu and Buddhist mandalas, Islamic mosques, and Catholic cathedrals have applied such sacred geometry. Likewise, specific wavelengths are emitted from the geometric forms and colors of the LifeParticle Sun image based on such principles.

Many phenomena and instances of healing with the LifeParticle Card have been reported by people who have used the LifeParticle Card. For example, if you place the card on a painful area, you get a feeling of stagnant energy moving there, accompanied by a decrease in the pain; or if you place the card on your chest when you sleep, your chest feels more comfortable and sleep comes more easily. Its action in activating energy, especially of the brain and pineal gland, is powerful. If you bring the card close to your forehead, the energy of that spot is quickly activated, bringing feelings of magnetism and a clearer vision of the light. The feeling of energy is amplified when you bring the card close, like a conductor through which electricity passes.

If you don't have a LifeParticle Card for this meditation, you can cut out and use the LifeParticle Card image in the back of this book for a temporary use or you can use one of your hands and feel the energy emitting from your palm.

To do the meditation, sit in a meditation posture and straighten your lower back. Hold the LifeParticle Card in one hand, placing the other hand on your knee. Bring the LifeParticle Card to about seven inches in front of your eyes and stare at the image of the LifeParticle Sun. Imagine the LifeParticle energy spreading out from the image of the LifeParticle Sun and entering your brain. Try to detect subtle changes in your brain energy.

Slowly and repeatedly bring the LifeParticle Card closer to your eyes and then move it farther away. The feeling of magnetism will increase, and you may detect more energy changes in your brain. This is Jigam training using the LifeParticle Card.

Now stop moving your hand and hold the card about three inches in front of your eyes. Close your eyes and imagine LifeParticle energy coming from the card, passing your Indang point, your third eye, and reaching your pineal gland. Slowly and repeatedly move the card closer to your eyes, then farther away. The magnetic feeling  will be amplified. When you feel an energy connection between the card and your brain, stop moving the card and hold it in front of your eyes, continuing to accept the LifeParticle energy into your brain. Do this for about 10 to 20 seconds as you imagine an energy channel opening up between your Indang point and your pineal gland.

Now use the same process to open all the major energy points of your brain—Junjung, Baekhwe, Noeho, Ahmun, and Taeyang. One by one, open up all these energy channels to your pineal gland.

Next move the LifeParticle Card around your head, slowly and freely, to open every area of your brain and face. Whenever the LifeParticle Card passes a point, imagine the energy of that spot being activated, as if a magnet were passing by.

Finally, bring the LifeParticle Card in front of your chest to boost the energy of your soul. If you move the card repeatedly back and forth in front of your chest or sweep the energy of your chest, making slow circles in front of it, the feeling of magnetism will grow stronger. Holding the card in front of you,

continue sending LifeParticles into your chest. You will feel your chest opening and becoming more comfortable.

Did you charge yourself with lots of LifeParticles? Some people have powerful energetic experiences on their first attempt; for others, the feeling of energy is still slight. Don't be in a hurry. It's only natural for there to be differences between people based on individual conditions, focus, and proficiency. Don't be discouraged after one attempt—with practice and concentration, anyone can feel it.

As preparation for full Pineal Gland Meditation, I recommend about 21 days of practicing connecting with your body (introduced in Chapter 6), connecting with your soul (introduced in Chapter 7), and activating the brain energy system (introduced in this chapter). Develop a sense for concentrating your awareness completely in your body, purifying the energy of your thoughts and emotions, and activating the pure energy in your heart and brain. Only then will you be ready to fully awaken your pineal gland to connect with your divinity.

I'll now guide you through the entire process of Pineal Gland Meditation—a practice for connecting with your divinity—from beginning to end. Some of you will be new to meditation, others skilled practitioners. If you think that you're not yet ready to have a deep experience, read through the following training methods first to help set a direction for your practice of Pineal Gland Meditation.

Full Flow of Pineal Gland Meditation

The first part of the flow is preparation, a process for activating the energy of the body and soul to create an energy body.

To prepare, relax your body with light stretching, and then sit in a meditation posture with your back straight.

Start with the first step of Pineal Gland Meditation as described in Chapter 6, connecting with your body. Do Belly Button Healing for about three minutes, controlling your breathing. Bring your outward-directed consciousness completely back into your body and internal consciousness.

Continue now to the second step as explained in Chapter 7, connecting with your soul. Close your eyes and do Jigam training, feeling the energy between your hands. Face your palms toward your chest, and activate the energy of your soul using the healing energy coming from your palms.

It's optional, but it will be most effective if you now do Aroma Energy Meditation and Sound Healing Meditation Level 2 (Jitalk) to expand your energy body. As you do Jitalk, try to express the feeling of your soul while very slowly moving your hands, going with the energy. Express with your hands and song, your soul's longing to encounter the light of divinity and become brighter, freer, and more peaceful. Visualize your emotions being purified, your soul energy passing the Soul Gate and rising into your head.

You are ready now for the third step, connecting with divinity. Slowly bringing your hands to the sides of your head, do Brain Jigam. Strengthen the sense of magnetism between your hands and your brain, repeatedly moving your hands close to and then away from your head. Once the feeling of magnetism becomes strong, moving your hands slowly, open up the major energy points on your head, one by one. Then move your hands freely, imagining that you are creating a helmet of energy around your head, to activate the energy of your entire brain.

I will now guide you in meditation for awakening the pineal gland to connect with divinity. Straighten your lower back once more. Slowly open your eyes and bring a LifeParticle Card in front of your eyes. Accept the energy coming from the LifePar-ticle Sun into your brain. Move the card toward and away from your face, creating and strengthening a feeling of magnetism around your brain. Then close your eyes and concentrate your mind on the LifeParticle Card. Visualize powerful LifeParticles continuing to enter your brain.

Then, bring the LifeParticle Card over the crown of your head without touching it, opening your Baekhwe point. Accept into the crown of your head the energy emitted from the LifeParticle Card. Imagine the energy of heaven entering your head and descending along your spine. Visualize a pillar of energy being set up from Heaven's Gate at the crown of your head to the Earth Gate at the bottom of your trunk. This pillar of energy is called the Heavenly Line, an energy line connecting your body to heaven. Likewise, energy rises from the ground, passing the Earth Gate and rising along your spine to your Heaven's Gate. This is called the Earth Line, the energy line connecting your body with the earth. Visualize the Heavenly Line and Earth Line meeting. With the strength of these two energy lines, you may feel your spine automatically straightening even more.

Using the LifeParticle Card, sweep your energy field very slowly down from the crown of your head along the centerline at the front of your body. Repeat this several times, strengthening the energy line. If energy somewhere in your body feels stagnant, hold the card over that area and focus intently on the area to direct energy there.

When you feel the energy of your whole body activating, bring the LifeParticle Card again in front of your eyes. Visualize bright, powerful LifeParticle energy shooting out of the card and entering your pineal gland through your Indang point. Like a magnifying glass focusing sunlight on a single spot, imagine energy coming from the LifeParticle Sun vibrating and awakening the energy of your pineal gland. Really spread your forehead by lifting its muscles upward, better enabling the light of LifeParticles to enter your brain.

Now, slowly put down the card on the floor and place your hands on your knees. With your eyes still closed, straighten your back and breathe deeply and slowly, feeling your soul in your heart. Then feel the location of the pineal gland in your brain. Imagine that your consciousness is there in your pineal gland. Hold your consciousness there until you have a sense of opening, clarity, or brightness—the eye of the pineal gland opening. Observe energy phenomena arising in front of your forehead as you continue to control your breathing. You might see light or feel pressure or a pulse in your forehead. Relax the muscles of your forehead. Allow yourself to slip into a peaceful, relaxed mindset, without hurrying.

Keep your heart wide open through deep breathing and just accept the light of LifeParticles coming into your pineal gland. Diverse phenomena may appear such as a single point of light, as small as a pinhole, that then perhaps gradually grows larger; or a bluish light may flicker or spread out or spin like a vortex. Various geometrical patterns may appear, moving as if dancing. Whatever its form or color, accept the energy of light into your pineal gland. Keep accepting it, keep opening up. The light will come into your brain, into your heart, eventually spreading into your whole body. Entrust yourself to the light. That light will soothe and heal your lonely and troubled heart, a heart that only wants to be loved.

That light is love. It's a blessing. It's complete love, love you couldn't have received from anyone, anywhere in the world. Accept that love deep into your heart. It's the light of life, the light of divinity, the light of heaven, loving you unconditionally. Without realizing it, you may shed tears as you are overwhelmed by that incredible love. Just accept it without hesitation. Fill your heart completely with that great love—and respond with "Thank you." Say, "Thank you. Thank you," expressing what's in your heart. "Thank you for loving me this much." The love sent by heaven fills your heart, fills your body, fills each and every cell—the energy of blessings fills you completely.

Slowly raise your hands to shoulder height, palms upward. Imagine the energy of heavenly blessings descending upon you. Fully open the Heaven's Gate in the crown of your head and accept that light. Brilliantly shining light will enter the crown of your head and spread through your body, transforming every cell into light. You are dwelling within light.

You are one with light. No, you are the light itself. As you practice, you may have the feeling that your brain and body, filled with light, have disappeared, or that your brain is expand-

ing to infinity—as if the boundary of your physical self has disappeared, as if you exist as light, as consciousness. That consciousness is the *spiritual body*.

Try to gradually expand your consciousness. Let your consciousness grow large enough to contain the cosmos. You will feel as if the whole universe is spreading out in all directions, centered on the being that is you—or, to be more precise, the consciousness that is you. You'll feel oneness, complete unity, a sense that you and the cosmos are one—a feeling that cannot be penetrated by any sense of separation.

Your consciousness, your brain, is one with the cosmic brain, cosmic consciousness—a massive, unified field—and at the same time a part of it. Your brain is connected with the cosmic brain. Your brain uploads and downloads information to and from this universal brain. You feel that everyone's brain is connected with the universal brain, just as you are. All of us are part of a brain interconnected as one, forming a single cosmic brain. The consciousness of each individual affects the cosmic brain, the cosmic consciousness and, on a smaller scale, the earth brain, the consciousness of humanity.

You and I are separate in the visible world, but we are all one, interconnected, in the world of consciousness. Our bodies are separate, but we are souls that have emerged, separating out from the massive One. Each of these souls has its own mission: uploading to the cosmic brain the information we feel and experience in our lives and downloading the information to actualize it into reality. For our common goal of upgrading the cosmic brain, each of us lives our life eagerly, crashing against obstacles, taking up challenges, and realizing many things. And we can access that uploaded information, sharing it.

We can meet the past, the present, and the future in our brains. We can connect with everything, from the information contained in the genes we received from our parents and ancestors to the history of humanity and the earth, and the principles of nature and the cosmos. That is the mystery of our brains, our consciousness. When you know how to connect your brain with the cosmic brain and download its information, you can escape from the narrow confines of yourself. You can download high-level information to the extent that your consciousness is connected with the cosmic brain—the way the data you can download on your computer is determined by the speed of your internet connection. Your channel for connecting to the cosmic brain is your pineal gland.

Pineal Gland Meditation brings fundamental changes to your consciousness. The underlying cause of your suffering has been your sense of separation and isolation. That's why you wanted to belong to something—to connect with the people you love, to form a family that would bring you stability of mind, to belong to a community, or to have a faith you could rely on. It was difficult to endure the separation and isolation you felt by not being connected with someone or belonging to something.

Through Pineal Gland Meditation, though, you experience a sense of complete oneness. The consolation of connection and belonging to the home of the soul, the source of eternal life, the cosmos—this feels indescribably deep and comforting. Great peace and security fill your heart, wrapping your body in the warmth of deep love and blessings, as if your soul is being embraced snugly in the loving arms of a cosmic parent, as if you've finally come to the home of your soul. The sense of separation and isolation disappears in an instant, your feelings of inadequacy vanishing. Within complete oneness, you can declare, "I am whole!"

In the unseen world of energy, in the world of consciousness, all are originally interconnected as one. You struggle merely because you have failed to realize this. Now all you need to do is be consciously aware of and connect with the divinity—the feeling of wholeness and oneness—within yourself. The secret is found in your brain and your pineal gland, in the domain of mystery. Through the process of Pineal Gland Meditation, may you open the secret door leading to the mysterious world of consciousness, to brighter and greater cosmic consciousness, to the world of unity.

CHAPTER 9

Guidelines for Pineal Gland Meditation

When you were a little kid, did you ever close your eyes and notice that you see much more than just darkness? A light show of neon flashes and dazzling starbursts may have appeared before your eyes. Try it now; you will probably still see it.

Seeing a light is one of the most common phenomena that Pineal Gland Meditation practitioners experience. If you think that what you're seeing may be natural daylight or light from indoor illumination, then try this experiment: Do Pineal Gland Meditation in a dark room, with the lights turned off and no light coming in from any other source. Most likely, you will still see the light from your pineal gland, even though it may sometimes be dim or vague.

Generally, during Pineal Gland Meditation, you'll see a light that's blue or white, or gold or other colors, taking on different patterns. You may see that light in your normal daily life when you're not seated meditating—when you're taking a shower or just kicking back, relaxing. You may also sense light flashing before your eyes at night after you turn off the lights and lie down to sleep. Sometimes you may see it even with your eyes open. This is a universal phenomenon of life and nature that occurs when the energy of the pineal gland is activated.

God, divinity, the Holy Spirit, light of eternal life, great white light, divine light—the names used in different spiritual traditions are merely different names for the same energy phenomena. Regardless of what it is called, we all experience something similar when in a meditative state, our mind calm and our pineal gland activated. This isn't some artificial happening in a particular religious sect or organization; it is a vital phenomenon that can be experienced by any human when their consciousness grows brighter.

In Pineal Gland Meditation, that light is called the "light of divinity" or the "LifeParticle Sun," meaning that it comes from the source of life energy. It has always been shining on us, transcending space and time. It was there before you were born, before the earth existed, and it will continue after you're gone, after the planet has disappeared. As the sun shines on the earth in the material world, so, too, the LifeParticle Sun shines on us in the spiritual world. The reason we have trouble feeling that light is simply that our sense for detecting it hasn't been activated. You will be able to detect the light of infinite love, blessings, and eternal life coming toward you once that sense is activated. And your soul will become one with the light of divinity, which it has been earnestly seeking. That is the moment of divine-human unity. Korea's ancient text, the *Sam Il Shin Go*, in its teachings on God, expresses it this way:

"God has already descended and dwells in your brain."

God dwells in us—but where? The *Sam Il Shin Go* points to a specific part of the human body: the brain! We experience connection with the light of divinity when our brain, and especially the pineal gland—has been activated. Modern brain science refers to "God in the brain." That an ancient Sundo text describes it this way is stunning.

In the flow of Pineal Gland Meditation, after encountering the light of divinity in our brain, we go one step beyond. The next step is opening wide Heaven's Gate in the crown of our head. As mentioned in the previous chapter, when Heaven's Gate is opened, you feel a pillar of brilliantly shining light pouring down into your whole body, entering through the crown of your head. Raising your arms at this time and receiving the blessing of that light, your consciousness rising, you feel as if your brain and body have disappeared, leaving you full of nothing but light. And you feel this awareness expanding to infinity, the universe spreading out in all directions. You experience the world of complete unity, being connected and one with cosmic consciousness—the feeling that you exist at the center of the universe.

There are expressions in Sundo that describe this ecstasy. One of these is found in the *Chun Bu Kyung*, Sundo's oldest text, containing in 81 characters all the principles of creation.

"The original mind of humanity is bright like the sun.
Pursuing brightness, you realize
that heaven and earth are one in humanity."

It describes a state in which your consciousness is one with the consciousness of the cosmos and in which the energy of the cosmos, the energy of heaven and earth, is entering and acting in you. I describe this as experiencing the *universal body*.

What you primarily perceive before you start Pineal Gland Meditation is just your physical body. Then you experience that body changing into the energy body as you stop your emotions, control your breathing, and feel energy. Next, when your soul energy encounters the light of divinity, your energy body is uplifted, becoming a spiritual body with a higher vibrational frequency. When cosmic energy enters you through

Heaven's Gate, your spiritual body is transformed, reaching the level of the universal body, which is one with the whole cosmos. This is the mystery of the human body, energy, and consciousness. Your body hasn't disappeared, but you're able to experience it on a higher level, one in which its energy and awareness are raised, transcending physical dimensions so that you become one with the universe. In Sundo, this is called Shinmyung, the state in which the shin energy of the upper dahnjon has been illuminated.

Think of this state as a bright light turning on in a dark room. The furniture and other objects, indistinguishable when the room was dark, are all clearly visible now. The illumination of consciousness is like this. When your consciousness is dim, you don't see the principles of the world or of life and are frustrated by not knowing what you should do. So you seek counsel from people with knowledge and experience in the areas you're concerned about; you expect them to be able to see what you can't.

However, in a state of Shinmyung, you have the capability to see what you should do yourself. The illumination of consciousness you experience in Shinmyung has been described as the opening of the third eye or the all-seeing eye—the eye that can see all things. This is different from your physical eyes. It means you've developed a broad vision for viewing the world from an awareness that is connected with cosmic consciousness. You have insight capable of seeing into all things and a sense of clarity as the fog blurring your vision is lifted. When you attain Shinmyung, you naturally realize the principles underlying the reality of humanity, the world, and the universe. You're able to transcend your limits and discover solutions to the problems that worry you. You can see yourself, others, and the world with a clearer and brighter consciousness.

Along with light, many people experience vibration when

they do Pineal Gland Meditation. This may come in a variety of forms. It is most commonly experienced first as a sense of pressure, as if something is pressing on the third eye point. You may feel as if you're wearing a headband, and you may feel a pulse between your eyebrows—like a fish opening and closing its mouth. Or you may experience subtle vibrations, a heavy pressure, or a cyclical pulse in the center of your brain. When your pineal gland is highly activated, you'll sense the center of your brain beating rapidly, like a hummingbird flapping its wings—its vibrations spreading through your body and beyond, transcending your physical boundaries.

Also, while doing Pineal Gland Meditation, there may be times when some scene or event experienced long ago will come to mind. You may sense that such memories are connected with a problem you're currently having, helping you to understand yourself better and escape from any self-judgment you may harbor. You may gain clues to the causes of problems in your relationships with the people around you or think of solutions.

These memories had been stored deep in your unconscious mind. Human mental activities encompass not only the conscious world we normally perceive and can control, but also an unconscious world we aren't normally aware of. Breathing, heartbeat, digestion, excretion, and other vital bodily functions of the human body, as well as survival-related needs such as food and sex, all arise in the unconscious mind.

Unconscious information is deep and vast. All the physical, emotional, and mental experiences of your entire life are recorded in your organs and cells, along with genetic information inherited from your parents, creating a record of all your joyful memories, emotional wounds, experiences of failure and rejection, and even stress. When faced with some new situation, you may find yourself having negative thoughts and feeling irrationally anxious or afraid, or being strangely repulsed by or attracted to someone. Logically inexplicable, these reactions come from the unconscious information stored in your body.

Have you ever heard of someone receiving a heart transplant and then suddenly showing the same personality, habits, and talents as the organ donor? We can assume from this that memories and information are stored in organs and cells, not just the brain. The dread, anxiety, fear, and other emotions recorded in our organs and cells suffuse our unconscious minds. That's why anxiety is difficult to consciously control once it develops. No matter how much we think, "I shouldn't be anxious," our anxiety doesn't disappear. In many cases it can't be resolved by drugs or psychological counseling. But after suffering for years from anxiety disorders that were only temporarily controlled by medication, many people have found relief after cleansing their emotions or memories through Pineal Gland Meditation.

How is this possible? Originally, our brain is connected with everything—the visible and invisible worlds, conscious and unconscious worlds, past and present, self and cosmos. However, we can't really integrate our brain when we're focused only on the visible world. When we go into our deep, internal consciousness through Pineal Gland Meditation, these previously disconnected and unperceived worlds are integrated, and memories buried deep in our unconscious—memories we don't normally perceive—come to the surface. Our brains want to recover their original, balanced condition. Healing comes to the unconscious mind when, in a meditative state, we recognize that our current problems are rooted in information from our past.

There's no need to deliberately bring any particular memories or emotions to mind when you do Pineal Gland Meditation. It's enough to let go of intentional thoughts and feelings, focusing instead on entering your internal consciousness. When the time comes, memories and information that require purification and balance will come up on their own. Deeper unconscious information will spread out before you, reflecting how far within yourself you've gone and how connected you now are with your inner world. The cleansing of your unconscious information will begin the moment you go within yourself through Pineal Gland Meditation.

I usually get this kind of question from people doing Pineal Gland Meditation: "Other people have mystical experiences, but I don't see any lights, and I don't seem to be making any progress in my meditation practice. What should I do?"

I have this advice for those with such worries: Set aside the rush, the habit of comparing yourself with others, and concentrate on *your soul*. Vibrations, images, or light seen during meditation are a kind of energy phenomenon. What's important is the essence, not the outward sign. What is the essence? It is your soul. Above all else, connect with the feeling in your heart, the feeling of your soul. Your practice will progress naturally if you focus there. Chasing mystical phenomena when you're not connected with your soul won't help you much; in fact, it's a vainglorious pursuit. How would seeing light or past lives or auras during meditation, without being connected to your essence, increase your quality of life, or that of anyone else?

If you are overly curious about esoteric phenomena, the balance becomes broken. Those who aren't firmly centered in their souls may suffer from visual or auditory hallucinations or be pulled so far into the mystical realms that it gets in the way of leading a healthy, balanced life. When your soul is your solid center, however, you can control any spiritual phenomena you experience. What's important is having your soul—your essence—as your foundation.

The key to awakening your pineal gland and attaining Shin-myung is to be found in your soul. Progress toward this state depends on how sincerely and earnestly your soul longs to encounter divinity, and on your sincere desire to grow and complete your soul. Have a deep longing for your consciousness to shine bright enough and broad enough to embrace all things. This consciousness is the heart that seeks the common good, which manifests as a highly developed form of social awareness. This is the pure energy of the soul. When that energy fills the heart, it can rise to the brain and awaken the energy of the pineal gland.

Don't be in a hurry, thinking, "Why don't I see the light? Why doesn't my pineal gland open?" Instead, try to have an attitude that says, "I want to grow the soul in my heart. I earnestly want my soul to encounter the light of divinity." When that intention grows stronger and stronger, your soul will enter the Heavenly Palace, even opening Heaven's Gate.

Expecting to experience all of this in one attempt is unrealistic. First you need to go faithfully through the process of connecting with your body, connecting with your soul, and activating your brain's energy. You can get help from trained instructors for these three steps at Body & Brain Yoga or online at ChangeYourEnergy.com.

No matter how busy you are, you can incorporate this process into your life. Sometimes you'll have plenty of time to focus calmly on Pineal Gland Meditation. At other times, you'll need to make some time to do it, even if it's not for very long. Choose the flow that's right for your situation.

Full Flow

This is the full meditation flow, encompassing the entire process, from connecting with your body to becoming one with cosmic consciousness. If you set a specific time frame for this—21 days, a month, 100 days, or whatever you decide—and practice regularly every day, you'll find yourself making noteworthy progress in the depth of your meditation experience.

1. Belly Button Healing (5 minutes, See Chapter 6)
Calling your consciousness into your body, sit in a meditative posture and do Belly Button Healing. Then, controlling your breathing, feel your breath sinking deeply and naturally into your lower abdomen.

2. Jigam Training (3 minutes, See Chapter 7)
Stop your emotions and calm yourself through Jigam training. Feel the energy between the palms of your hands, and send that energy into your chest, boosting the energy of your soul. Imagine your physical body becoming an energy body.

3. Aroma Energy Meditation (optional, 1 to 2 minutes, See Chapter 7)
To strengthen your energy body, apply Bird of the Soul oil or another aromatic oil such as lavender, peppermint, sage, or rosemary to the third-eye point, the tip of your nose and the inside of your wrists. Bring your wrist in front of your nose and smell the fragrance. Imagine the aroma spreading through your brain and your body, changing it into an energy body.

4. Sound Healing Meditation: Jitalk (optional, 3 minutes, See Chapter 7)

Use Jitalk sound meditation to express the longing of your soul to be brighter and freer by encountering divinity. Imagine the Soul Gate in your throat opening and the energy of your soul rising into your Heavenly Palace.

5. Activating Brain Energy (3 minutes, See Chapter 8)
Now do Brain Jigam. Feeling the energy between your hands and brain, open your brain's energy points and activate its energy. You can use the LifeParticle Card to do this.

6. Pineal Gland Meditation (5 to 10 minutes, See Chapter 8)
Using a LifeParticle Card, open and establish your energy line from the crown of your head to your perineum. Next bring the card in front of your forehead, visualizing LifeParticle energy entering your pineal gland. When you have a magnetic feeling in your brain, lower the card and meditate, focusing on your pineal gland.

Concentrating on the feeling of the soul in your heart, breathe and connect with the light of divinity shining on your pineal gland from in front of your eyes.

Next, open wide Heaven's Gate in the crown of your head, accepting the energy of heaven. Feeling the bright energy pouring down into your whole body, experience oneness with cosmic consciousness. If you have an issue to solve, you can ask your brain to find the solution. Finally, meditate as you visualize in detail your hope and vision becoming reality. Close with a prayer of sincere gratitude.

Short Flow

With this flow, you take just a little time for simple meditation using the LifeParticle Card. This is good when you want to connect with your inner self and awaken your brain, increasing your focus.

1. Belly Button Healing (3 minutes, See Chapter 6)
Doing Belly Button Healing for a moment before meditation is even more effective, since it causes you to breathe more deeply, from your lower abdomen. But if the overall energy of your body is relatively balanced, it's fine to go directly into meditation without doing Belly Button Healing, or after doing some simple stretching.

2. Activating Brain Energy (3 minutes, See Chapter 8)
Bring the LifeParticle Card in front of your open eyes. Charge your brain and awaken your pineal gland using the energy coming in from the card. Close your eyes and use the LifeParticle Card to open and establish your energy line, slowly sweeping the card several times from the crown of your head down to your perineum.

3. Pineal Gland Meditation (5 minutes, See Chapter 8)
Bringing the LifeParticle Card in front of your forehead, visualize LifeParticle energy going into your pineal gland. When you are aware of a magnetic feeling in your brain, lower the card and meditate, focusing on your pineal gland.

Note: If you're meditating without a LifeParticle Card, close your eyes and establish your energy line, sweeping one hand several times from the crown of your head to your perineum. Now bring your palm in front of your forehead and do Brain

Jigam to strengthen the feeling of magnetism in your brain. Then, concentrate on your pineal gland as you meditate.

One characteristic distinguishing Pineal Gland Meditation from other meditative methods is that it makes use of tools that are readily available to anyone. The Healing Life tool is one of these; by using it to do Belly Button Healing for just a few minutes, your consciousness will focus in your body and your breathing will deepen and sink into your lower abdomen. The second tool is the LifeParticle Card, a wonderful means of quickly creating a feeling of magnetism in your body, especially your brain and pineal gland. Yet another tool is Bird of the Soul Essential Oil, which instantly refreshes your brain and puts you in a good mood, helping you develop your energy body. Using these tools decreases the time it takes your consciousness to enter a meditative state and helps increase your concentration and the depth of your meditation. You can learn more about these tools at ConnectbyIlchi.com. Again, if you don't have these tools, you can use your hands or other available alternatives.

If you want deep experiences of energy and consciousness and life change, I recommend deciding on a set period and doing the Full Flow with devotion. If you don't have the time for that, try to take time to close your eyes and meet your inner self every day, if only for a moment or two. We all need a time for coming back within and being completely one with ourselves. Only then can we connect with and live as our true selves.

What does it mean to lead a spiritual life? Spirituality won't find a place in our lives just because we light candles and incense or decorate our bodies and rooms with accessories advertising our esoteric interests. A genuine spiritual life begins when you connect with your true self. It's living your own life, not being dragged around by your preconceptions and emotions or putting others' opinions and expectations of you first. To live a truly spiritual life, you need to take time at least once a day to bring your vision inward, to connect with your true self, your attention having been focused outside all day. Through this time you can meet and talk with yourself, and possibly even get hints or answers about your worries. This is a time for imbuing yourself with vitality. It's a time for loving yourself by focusing your attention on your soul—a soul that has been disheartened by all sorts of thoughts, feelings, and stresses.

A spiritual life is one in which you change your life by connecting with yourself every day, boosting your soul's energy. The good effects of this will expand even to the people around you. Won't you start such a spiritual life?

PART III

Additional Pineal Gland Meditation Methods

CHAPTER 10

Five Steps to Becoming the Master of Your Brain

Now I want to introduce the principles and innovative methods of Brain Education. Along with the Korean tradition of Sundo, these are the principles on which Pineal Gland Meditation is based. Brain Education is very closely connected with Jungchoong, Kijang, and Shinmyung from Sundo, as previously explained. I especially emphasized the Shinmyung level and combined that with the discoveries of modern neuroscience when I developed Brain Education. The goal is to help everyone make the best use of their brain's power in their everyday life. In this section, you can examine your consciousness and understand the flow of your life and the world through the concepts of Brain Education.

I often ask audiences a question when I start a lecture on Brain Education.

"Did you bring your brain with you today?"

Breaking out in laughter, they all answer in a loud voice, "Yes!" Of course they've brought their brains. "Really?" I ask them. "Are you sure you haven't left your brain somewhere else? Shouldn't you take back your brain?" Still laughing, they begin to wonder about the real intention of my question. Aren't you also curious about what it means?

Of course, we always have our brains with us, 24 hours a day. That is the brain on a physical level. But are we really aware of our brains? Are we living as their masters? We carry our physical brains with us, but don't we often forget about them and move around without noticing them? Are we leaving our brains somewhere else, entrusting them to someone else? While we may be the masters of our brains physically, we've actually left the position of master in the hands of others. I'll give you a few examples.

First of all, our brains are often habitually addicted to something external. For example, we may be unable to extricate ourselves from things such as games, television, alcohol, tobacco, other drugs, shopping, or foods. If something you start doing to relieve your brain's boredom or stress takes over your brain, moving beyond your control, that can be considered an "addiction."

Intense experiences can make a clear impression on the brain through neurochemical stimulation such as dopamine secretion, and feelings of pleasure, excitement, and satisfaction. Then, the brain may repeatedly search for those same intense feelings, which causes the formation of an addiction. When you continuously chase after temporary pleasures, stress relief, or reality avoidance, the pain you are escaping from builds up, you are unable to focus on your present life. Body and mind become exhausted and impoverished. If your brain is being led about in this way, you need to act quickly to take back your brain.

Another situation is when your brain is captured by a negative consciousness that you yourself have created. For example, you might continuously interpret some past event in a way that debilitates you, leaving you unable to pull yourself out of an endless cycle of self-recrimination. This kind of victim consciousness could be called a form of mental addiction, one that captures the brain. You interpret yourself, other people, and life from the perspective of victim consciousness, blaming your environment and saying that things happen "because of you" or "because of that." In this way, you try to justify your own weakness and limited consciousness, which makes it difficult to make balanced judgments. When you have a negative view of yourself, you keep pulling yourself down, constantly reminding yourself that you're ugly or stupid, incompetent, unworthy of love. As you repeat and expand the circuits of such negative thinking, they slowly form rigid structures in your brain.

This kind of self-image is bound to have an effect on the perspective with which you view other people and the world. When you're depressed, the world also looks depressed, and when you're happy, the world looks happy. If your brain is stuck in a morass of emotions such as depression, anxiety, inferiority feelings, and self-contempt, you need to pull your brain out of this pattern quickly. Don't mortgage your brain to such forms of information.

External information may also capture your brain. Personal relationships, for example, are a source of information. Your parents, siblings, spouse, friends, and workplace colleagues all give you information that contributes to your sense of self and perception of the world. Have you ever been suddenly, intensely angered by words they've said, especially criticisms of you? If so, your brain has been totally captured by that information. Once you understand this, you realize that these are merely *their* opinions, bits of information created by *their* brains. But *your* brain has absorbed those words unfiltered, as if they were absolute truths.

Examine yourself to see whether you're stuck in the information you've received from the people around you. Are you evaluating yourself and your life according to those words? If so, you need to take back your brain. Look directly at this reality: your brain is being controlled by the information others have given you, whether they intended that or not. The master of your brain should be you, not them. Don't let other people use your brain without your permission.

Various systems of society also provide external information that has a significant impact on our brains. Information we get from our school, workplace, government, religion, social values, ethics, morals, popular culture, and commercial advertising, and the like—it's a mishmash of information that flows into our brains haphazardly. Our belief systems and value systems are formed based on such information. Here are some examples. Bewitched by corporate advertising, you consume too much. Or, under the influence of biased news media, you divide people into Us and Them, disparaging the other side, aligning yourself with the ideology of some politician or political party. Frankly, such social systems are misappropriating our brains. If we're allowing that to happen, then whose brains are they, really? Is it your brain or theirs? If you really stop to think about the fact that you have handed over your brain to them, you will probably be stunned. I hope that you will be thunderstruck by that awareness so that you start taking back your brain now. Face the truth: it is you, not them, who has neglected your brain and allowed others to use it without your permission.

Generally our brains are absorbed in pursuing value that is considered important by society—in other words, "social value." We think that our existential value is recognized through our social value. We have to be successful, earn a lot of money, rise to high status, develop our skills and appearance—and we have to stake our lives on this. Of course, social value is important to social animals like us. But we need to remember that social value isn't everything. If you think social value is the be-all and end-all of your existence, you won't be able to escape from anxiety, worry, and fear. Within the framework of ceaseless comparison and competition—feeling that you have to do better, have more, and be better off than others—you end up struggling and worrying, fearful that your social value might drop below that of others. Social value based on comparison and competition can never bring us genuine satisfaction.

True inner satisfaction comes from discovering absolute values—ones you choose yourself, not those determined for you by society or other people. Discover your own inner worth, a value that does not need to be—that cannot be—compared with anyone who is not you. It's not a value that can be found in the visible, finite world. Rather, it's an infinite and incomparable value, an absolute value you can encounter when you focus within yourself. Those who discover this value can live their own authentic lives, not lives expected of them or imposed on them by society or other people. That is what it means to take back your brain.

I created Brain Education out of a passionate desire to help anyone take back their brain and live as its master. Brain Education is made up of these five steps:

Step 1—Brain Sensitizing
Step 2—Brain Versatilizing
Step 3—Brain Refreshing
Step 4—Brain Integrating
Step 5—Brain Mastering

Linking this with the Pineal Gland Meditation described in this book, Steps 1 and 2 correspond to the process of connecting with your body, Step 3 corresponds to connecting with your soul, and Step 4 corresponds to connecting with your divinity.

When your brain is integrated through this last step, your life of Brain Mastering begins. Here is the process of mastering your brain in detail.

Step 1 of Brain Education, Brain Sensitizing, is about awakening your ability to be aware of your body and brain. Your attention has mainly been directed outward until now, so in this step you learn to call that attention inward, toward yourself. You develop a new awareness and say to yourself, "Ah, I have a body and a brain." Not only do the five senses of the body become heightened, but you awaken a new "sixth sense," the feeling of energy. Through various exercises that move the body, including yoga-like stretching, you discover where your body's balance is disrupted and where energy flow is blocked as you increase your awareness of your body and brain.

When your awareness awakens, you enter into the step of making your body and brain flexible through various physical and mental exercises. Brain Education Step 2, Brain Versatilizing, involves releasing stress and tension from your body and brain and using them in new ways. Your brain is "stiff" when your body and mind are tense. Through exercise and relaxation techniques, you learn to release the accumulated tension and stress, and thus your health begins to recover. And through these exercises you can make new connections both within your brain and between your brain and your body.

For example, when you move your body in new ways, you may find some movements awkward or uncomfortable. You may notice that inertia and old habits have been guiding your thinking and movement based on what has become ingrained in your body over a long period of time. If you keep moving, thinking, and acting differently through Brain Versatilizing exercises, you can break out of your current patterns and begin to think and act outside the box as your brain becomes more and

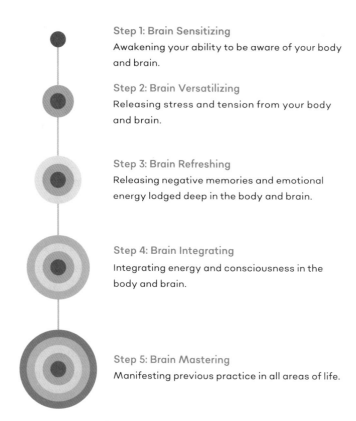

Step 1: Brain Sensitizing
Awakening your ability to be aware of your body and brain.

Step 2: Brain Versatilizing
Releasing stress and tension from your body and brain.

Step 3: Brain Refreshing
Releasing negative memories and emotional energy lodged deep in the body and brain.

Step 4: Brain Integrating
Integrating energy and consciousness in the body and brain.

Step 5: Brain Mastering
Manifesting previous practice in all areas of life.

The Five Steps of Brain Education

more flexible. In the process, you grow new connections between nerve cells, a capability known as neuroplasticity. As your thinking becomes more versatile, your conscious cognitive processes—handled by the cerebral cortex, or thinking brain, in the outermost part of the brain—become enhanced.

The next step addresses the limbic system, or the emotional brain, located below the cerebral cortex. When you go deep inside yourself, you come face to face with debilitating emotional memories and information. You realize that emotional baggage—such as old resentments and attachments—is impeding your growth and preventing the fulfillment of your latent potential, and that this is the underlying cause of your physical and mental problems. Once your brain realizes that, it naturally starts to let go of those emotional clots. Brain Refreshing, Step 3 of Brain Education, releases memories and emotional energy lodged deep in the body and brain. After you detoxify your emotional energy, you are able to adopt a positive perspective and handle future challenges more effectively.

As you progress through the second and third steps of Brain Education, you deal with your thinking brain and then your emotional brain. Finally, as the pineal gland awakens in the brainstem, the deepest part of the brain, a process of integration take place. In Step 4 of Brain Education, Brain Integrating, energy and consciousness are integrated in the body and brain. Energetic integration in the brain refers to smooth circulation of energy in the various areas of the brain—specifically, the left and right hemispheres and the three-layered structure consisting of the cerebral cortex, the limbic system, and the brainstem.

This is when you'll feel a state of peace and equilibrium—the original distinguishing feature of the brain. Energetic integration in the body means that the three energy centers in the brain, chest, and abdomen are strongly connected as one like a pillar of energy. Separate thoughts (brain), emotions (chest), and desires (abdomen) are integrated and simplified in one direction. At the same time, things outside of you that previously felt separate now connect as one and a great integration of consciousness comes, resulting in a sense of complete oneness.

When Brain Integration is achieved, you attain an egoless state called *muah*. According to a surface-level, literal interpretation, muah means "there is no me," but what it really means is that you transform from the small self of ego into a self that is connected as one with all things. Extraneous thoughts and emotions disappear, and you experience a state of clear and quiet peace, as though your brain is completely empty and refreshed. But it's not a hollow emptiness. It's a condition of being filled with the energy of life. It is from this state of muah that true creation arises. When you are in the state of muah, you come to the realization that you are capable of creating anything. That's when you can become the true master of your brain, and that's the ultimate goal of Brain Education. Step 5, Brain Mastering, goes beyond the level of meditation and training by practicing how to use the power of creation and your true self to manifest what you want in your daily life.

Brain Education is being taught at Body & Brain Yoga centers and also through academic systems. A PhD program in Brain Education is available at the International Graduate University of Brain Education in South Korea, and Brain Education is being implemented through the International Brain Education Association (IBREA), which has special Consultative Status with the United Nations Economic and Social Council. Brain Education has been incorporated into school systems throughout South Korea, the United States, Japan, Europe, and Central America, especially in El Salvador.

In that country, the changes observed in students are so significant that Brain Education is being taught in a quarter of all public schools. The children, who had been affected by gang violence, have certainly recovered hope and laughter through Brain Education, and the thousands of instructors who have become Brain Education trainers have been experiencing the benefits, too—including improved health, reduced stress, and better emotional control. These are the positive changes that occur when you become the master of your brain and enhance your power to manage your body and mind.

For Brain Mastering, identifying the current state of your brain needs to come first. I'm in the habit of explaining brain state by using three general categories: Dark Brain, Power Brain, and Divine Brain. To determine which of these describes the condition of your brain, start by asking yourself the following simple question.

"Am I positive and hopeful, or am I negative and pessimistic?"

Which is closer to your current state? The condition of your brain is the state of your consciousness, emotions, and energy. It may rise and fall several times a day, whenever your internal or external situation changes. However, people usually remain in a certain state of awareness and emotion. They have a zone of consciousness to which they keep returning, a kind of base camp. What emotional state is the base camp of your consciousness? Is your awareness generally positive and hopeful? Or is it negative and pessimistic?

I call a brain with positive consciousness a Power Brain. Conversely, a brain with negative consciousness is what I call a Dark Brain. A Dark Brain is a brain stuck in a state of negative awareness, characterized by shame, victim consciousness, fear, guilt, self-loathing, feelings of inferiority, anxiety, depression, lethargy, sadness, resentment, or anger. Try to imagine that your brain is in such a state right now; you're ashamed, fearful, and lethargic. Just imagining this makes your mind darker and heavier, doesn't it? Do you feel the strength seeming to leave your body? Remaining in a Dark Brain state is a path to continuously making yourself weaker. And it doesn't stop there, because it makes things hard for the people around you, too. Not only does that weak, heavy, dark energy infect those around you, but you end up constantly trying to feed off the energy of others to make up for your lack.

If you're in a Dark Brain state, you should get out of it as quickly as possible! Face it: your brain, caught by negative energy, can't budge. Continue like that and you'll inevitably find yourself stuck in a deep pit. Quickly wake up, pay attention, and take back your brain! You, not such emotions, are the master of your brain. Boldly and confidently declare that your brain is your own, and exercise your rights of ownership.

Masters have duties as well as rights. To be the master of your brain, you need to fulfill your duties and responsibilities as its owner. Begin by resolving to do just that:

"I am responsible for my life and the condition of my brain!"

Declare this right now. Say it sincerely and loudly to your brain, repeating your resolution three times. How does that feel? Don't you feel your brain awakening, its power growing? Being a Power Brain starts with clearly choosing that you will take responsibility for your life. Not passively waiting for others or the external environment to change your life, you pledge to change it proactively yourself. It means having a strong sense of ownership, a feeling that you are the master of your life—and that consequently everything about it is your own responsibility.

As you read this, once again try to get a sense for the feelings in your brain and body. Don't they seem to be getting stronger, brighter, more positive? A Power Brain gives off an energy capable of bringing bright, positive changes to others as well as to yourself. Its consciousness is characterized by qualities such as spontaneity, confidence, courage, acceptance, openness, understanding, tolerance, care, hope, love, compassion, gratitude, happiness, and joy. Quite a contrast with the consciousness of a Dark Brain, isn't it?

"Which is better, a Dark Brain or a Power Brain?" When asked this, anyone would choose the latter—and they'd want to know how they can be a Power Brain. This is my answer:

"It's purely and entirely up to you. You can be a Power Brain
right now if you but choose to be!"

Don't underestimate your brain, for it can draw on enormous power. And your brain is already equipped with everything it needs. It is ready to experience the full spectrum of consciousness, from shame and guilt to the heights of enlightenment. The human brain is capable of experiencing a fall into the hell of victim consciousness in one moment, feeling the hatred of everyone in the world, only to rise in another moment and experience lofty, pure love for all life. Our consciousness is like a light shining moment by moment. What mode of consciousness you choose and activate is up to you as the master of your own brain.

Of course, if you're just letting your brain be, having given up on becoming its master, it will not be able to operate at this level. Just as you use and manage your smartphone every day, shouldn't you be able to use and handle your brain properly if you are its master? You likely take great care of your smartphone. If you aren't just as interested in the condition of your own brain, it will be hard for you to manifest its infinite power, potential, and creativity.

Continuous choosing and practicing are required to be a Power Brain. Just because you've had a moment filled with confidence and hope, that condition won't continue forever. You may go back to a Dark Brain state, pushed there by the inertia of habits ingrained in your body as you've lived your life. There's no other way out but to honestly check the condition of your brain. "My brain is now a Dark Brain," you realize. "Negative consciousness is occupying my brain again." Then you can choose whether to continue in that state or get yourself out of it. Isn't it fortunate that you have been given the power and authority to make that choice at any moment, no matter how difficult or troubling your situation may be?

A Power Brain is someone who has clearly realized this: "I am responsible for my life and the condition of my brain!" Don't push that responsibility off onto anyone else, and don't make any excuses. Choose this harsh truth, and choose it over and over again. Practice, and then practice again. They say that a baby usually toddles stably only after falling down and getting back up about 1,500 times. To achieve brain mastery, it's only natural that innumerable attempts, trial and error, and continuous choosing and practice are necessary.

Pineal Gland Meditation is a shortcut that allows us to vertically raise the base camp of our awareness from Dark Brain to Power Brain. It allows consciousness to jump several levels at once instead of rising step by step. How is that possible?

When you enter deep meditation, you'll clearly see the current state of your consciousness. You'll realize what has captured your brain. You'll see that the forms of negative consciousness I've listed previously are actually heavy baggage continuously pulling you down. You can't help but be shocked when you see yourself holding tightly to such things, even though all you have to do is let go. Why? It's because those things are *delusions*. No real answers are found there, no matter how much you cling to them. You will just spin endlessly through a repeating circuit, going back and forth between suffering and pleasure.

If you tell people to let go of those delusions, though, they often act as if it's so hard that it's going to kill them. That's because they are comfortable only if they are holding onto something. Living that way has become a habit. They don't realize that they need to hold onto something else instead of what they've been grasping. What should you hold onto? There is but one answer: your true self, your original nature! This is your soul, and the divinity your soul wants so much to meet.

That alone is true and everlasting.

Becoming a Power Brain is a process of escaping from negative consciousness and awakening to the light and brilliance of your true nature. You can find significant help for this process through Pineal Gland Meditation. Of course, people who haven't meditated can experience the positive consciousness of a Power Brain, one that is characterized by confidence, courage, tolerance, understanding, and love. This is because you can become a Power Brain through conscious choice, effort, and will. To reach the next stage beyond Power Brain, though, there are limits to how far you can get through will and effort alone. You must enter the deep domain of your unconscious mind to definitely awaken your true nature. I call the brain that has experienced such enlightenment a Divine Brain.

Divine Brain is a state in which the divine nature in your brain has awakened. It means experiencing a sense of wonder, one in which your soul is fully connected and one with the divine nature of the cosmos. Through that feeling of oneness, your sense of separation disappears and a sense of belonging and deep comfort surrounds you—as if you've been embraced, having returned to the home of your soul. You tremble with energy of a high frequency, an energy of peace, infinite love, gratitude, and joy.

It's true that a Power Brain also feels peace, love, gratitude, and joy. But a Divine Brain is different in that these things become unconditional. Generally our brains feel joy and peace when certain conditions are satisfied, only to experience a loss of those emotions—the feelings vanishing like a puff of smoke—when our situation changes. A Divine Brain, though, is simply joyful, simply peaceful, without any external conditions being met. The quiet waters of peace, love, and joy that come from a sense of unity and connection with the Source continuously flow deep, deep within. They don't result from achieving or obtaining something. They come from having a true realization and opening of our eyes, from encountering the life that always exists—here and now, in this moment.

In Sundo, the state of the Divine Brain is called Shinin Hapil (divine-human unity), meaning that the true nature and divinity of humanity have become one. Most people consider this state to be somehow of a higher dimension, special and virtually unattainable. But that isn't the true meaning of the Divine Brain I'm talking about. I believe that anyone and everyone can, and should, become a Divine Brain. In fact, this is our brain's true and original nature.

Our brains are originally peaceful, for their nature is one of peace and equilibrium. Imagine a child laughing cheerfully. That child's brain is incomparably peaceful, still untouched by negative, limiting information. As we grow up, though, the brain's sense of peace and equilibrium becomes dull. In this condition, competing, clashing, disparaging, fighting, grabbing, and dominating bits of information have occupied our brains. Driven by such information, we laugh and cry and rage, we like and dislike, and we love and hate. The original state of our brains is gradually forgotten.

To return to this state, you must recover your brain's original senses. These aren't strange new senses that you introduce from somewhere else. Rather, it's the reawakening of senses that you've had within you since the time you were born.

The method for awakening these forgotten senses is *emptying*—emptying your brain of the countless bits of clashing information that have been ruling it. This means watching and emptying yourself of artificial thoughts, feelings, and desires, information crammed into you by the world as well as information you've created yourself. When I say to empty yourself, I'm saying to not be attached and bound to that information.

Realize that the information is illusory and delusional, and be free from it. The process for doing this is the spiritual practice of Jigam, Joshik, and Geumchok, described in detail in previous chapters, and the first through third steps of Brain Education.

When we empty ourselves again and again and again, the brain's original character—its sense for peace and equilibrium—starts to recover. The static that once echoed noisily in the brain stops, and we begin to gain a state of pure awareness. This is a state of egolessness, muah, which allows us to encounter the bright light of divinity in our brains. Imagine your brain shining brightly, having recovered peace and equilibrium. That bright light—life energy—fills the Heavenly Palace in the brain. This is the original character of your brain, its divine nature.

Divine nature isn't found only in special people. It's not something you can experience only if you go to a certain house of worship, read scriptures, and believe the right thing. Anyone whose brain is operating normally can experience it. Half god and half beast, human nature itself includes divinity. When you focus on your true nature, going ever inward, you will come face to face with your divine nature in the depths of your oceanic consciousness. And you will realize that the divine nature is interconnected and one with all things. The ancient Korean scripture *Sam Il Shin Go* expresses how to meet the divinity like this:

"Shouting, being drunk on energy, wishing, and praying do not allow you to meet the divine. Find the seed of divinity in your true nature. It has already descended and dwells in your brain."

I can't agree more. Divinity is a unique characteristic of humanity. Thus anyone can discover it if they concentrate on their true nature. To recover and connect with human nature and human character is the reason we were born in human form, and that is our true value as human beings. We should concentrate on recovering and protecting that value.

The systems of the world, though, seem to be going in the opposite direction. Instead of helping people find their true value and connect with themselves, it breaks that connection and encourages them to grow more distant from themselves. These systems include politicians who agitate and spread propaganda, claiming that only their ideologies and policies will make the world a better place; some narrow-minded religious leaders who still plant the consciousness of separation and discrimination, crying out that salvation is possible only through their belief systems; economic systems that encourage people to concentrate on external, material values and consumption rather than internal beauty and growth; and educational systems that ignore true holistic, creative learning, driving students to memorize standardized knowledge and compete. As we live our days immersed in such systems, it is only natural for our brains to be tainted by them.

In a democracy, the people rule. A genuine democracy, I think, is a society in which the true value of humanity is realized. It should help citizens discover the true nature of humanity and recover their original state of peace and equilibrium, not focus on agitating the public for the sake of some politician, political party, or ideology. Wouldn't true peace begin to find its place in the world if all of us recovered a sense for peace in our brains? A world where that is realized could be considered a genuine democracy.

There's something we should not overlook: our brains are the unique domain of the Creator, a domain no one else can possess. No authoritarian individual or organization, and no religion, can own that divine nature. The system of religion is a man-made construct. Our brains, on the other hand, are works of nature. The human brain existed before religious systems appeared in human history. Divinity didn't come to exist because of religions. It has always existed in our brains. Religion is just a tool, a method for helping us connect with divine nature. The absolute value is the divinity dwelling in our brains.

Do not ignore this problem any longer, allowing your brain to be used by society's systems without your permission. And don't just blame the systems, either. Each of us must open the eyes of our pineal gland, face the truth directly, and take back our brains. Please don't speak, act, or use energy in a way that pulls you and others down into a Dark Brain state. And never go with the flow of the world when it leads you to a Dark Brain. Live your own authentic life, boldly tearing to shreds the pictures drawn for you by others or by society, by those claiming that "this is your life." All the answers are found inside you—in your brain.

CHAPTER 11

Find Your Healing Points

I would like to introduce two methods of meditation that will allow you to experience the process of Brain Education in a short period of time, from Step 1, Brain Sensitizing, to Step 5, Brain Mastering. One of them, which I'll introduce in this chapter, is the BHP Energy Healing method. BHP stands for Brain Education Healing Points. The other one, Heaven's Gate Meditation, is explained in the following chapter. These two methods can be practiced separately, but if you do BHP Energy Healing right before you do Heaven's Gate Meditation, you will likely have a deeper experience.

BHP Energy Healing improves energy circulation in the body and helps the body's energy balance by using direct stimulation to open energy points. This is possible because brain and body are interconnected through a neural network and energy system.

Our brains and bodies are intricately connected. Key functions for maintaining our lives—including respiration, digestion, heartbeat, and body temperature—are performed automatically, without our conscious control. Our brains communicate with the relevant organs through our autonomic nervous system. We also don't really need to worry about sitting, standing, or other ordinary movements, because these are subconsciously controlled through our brains. Even walking, which seems very simple, is a complex symphony of sophisticated command and control, the nervous system orchestrating the interactions of hundreds of bones and muscles and thousands of nerves. Our brains process much more information than we're aware of, coordinating innumerable actions taking place in our bodies. Through BHP Energy Healing, we consciously take part in this communication between body and brain—finding energy healing points and stimulating them appropriately, inducing our bodies to heal themselves.

The first step of this method is to find your BHPs—your healing points. This is easy. Just find the places that hurt when pressed. Pain is a signal our bodies send to our brains to let them know that there is a problem. We normally don't worry much about our bodies—not until we experience discomfort or unusual symptoms such as severe fatigue.

BHP Energy Healing doesn't directly stimulate areas that are already clearly painful, such as places where you have joint or muscle pain. It finds the hidden pain points, the ones you don't normally recognize. From the perspective of energy, pain points are places where the flow of energy is blocked or stagnant. The aim of BHP Energy Healing is to stimulate these spots, treating them as trigger points to break through a series of energy blockages and improve energy circulation to other places in need of healing.

Although BHPs can be found in other areas as well, it's most immediately and powerfully effective to find and heal them in the scalp, fingers, and toes. When you do BHP Energy Healing for a while, you'll get a real feel for how closely different areas of our bodies are connected. Pressing one part of your scalp may relieve pain in your shoulders, or pressing the area around the nail of your middle finger may alleviate a headache and make your vision brighter. This is because your body is interconnected by a single neural network and energy system.

Finding Your BHPs

First look for BHPs on your scalp. Use either a blunt tool or your fingernails; don't use anything that's too pointed and might injure your skin. If using your fingernails, your thumbnail is the most effective; your index and middle fingers will also work. Your fingernails or tool should be clean, and you should avoid pressing any area where there is an open sore. Begin at the top of your head and work your way down toward the sides and back, pressing here and there on your scalp.

What feelings do you get? You may feel a refreshing sense of pressure in some places, or you may find spots that really hurt. Look for the places that hurt when you press them. Some spots may hurt so much when pressed that you find yourself letting out an "Ow!" These are your BHPs.

You'll usually have a few or many BHPs. It's different for every person, and it may be different depending on your condition on a particular day. BHPs can be classified according to pain intensity. Some points may be extremely painful, others moderately painful, and still others only slightly painful. Center your healing on the most severe pain points first, gradually moving out from there to other points.

Next look for BHPs in your fingers and toes. As shown in the image below, use your thumbnail or a tool to carefully press the areas around the cuticles of your fingernails and toenails. You're again looking for the places that hurt the most—your BHPs.

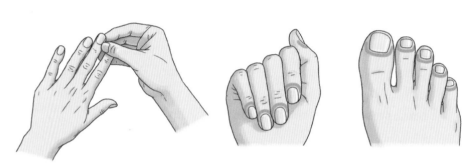

Once you've found a BHP, start your energy healing by stimulating this point. Press and release it, gently and repeatedly, for about a minute. After you've healed one spot, go on to the next. Adjust the intensity of your pressing as needed—it shouldn't hurt too much. Heal the spots with the most intense pain whenever you have the time, about three to five times a day.

BHP Energy Healing isn't only an effective method for restoring balance of the neural network and energy system; it's also a powerful method of meditation to experience the five steps of Brain Education, because it strengthens the connection between body and brain. The point is to make your brain aware of the entire process of healing. BHP Energy Healing is not just pressing the pain points a few times, but closing your eyes and observing your body, making your brain aware of exactly how your body is getting better and how your energy is changing. You are turning your brain into a control tower to oversee the detailed process of change in your body. Making your brain fully aware of the body is a great meditation for connecting body and brain.

BHP Energy Healing and Meditation

Now I'll guide you through the process of practicing BHP Energy Healing, and I'll explain how you can link it naturally with Pineal Gland Meditation.

Sitting in a meditative posture, close your eyes and bring your awareness into your body. Try to feel the condition of your body and mind. Do you have the feeling that energy is circulating well in your body right now? Does your mind feel light and bright, or does it feel a little heavy? Let your brain scan your body and mind. When you've accurately identified your present condition, you'll be better able to immerse yourself in BHP Energy Healing, and you'll be able to compare your feelings after healing with how you felt before.

Gently press the BHPs you found when you pressed your scalp. It will be painful and you will find yourself frowning. Brain Education Step 1, Brain Sensitizing, begins as soon as you press a BHP. Your brain goes "Whoa!" and is taken completely by surprise as it awakens. Your cognitive ability instantaneously shoots up. And you realize that the pain from that point is the stagnation of energy caused by tension and stress. Releasing that stress is Step 2 of Brain Education, Brain Versatilizing.

It might hurt so much that you want to stop. How, can you lessen the pain? The way to do this is to breathe out through your mouth. Test it once. First press a BHP with your mouth closed; then, again pressing your BHP, slightly open your mouth and slowly exhale through your mouth, "Hoo . . ." You'll be able to feel a difference.

Do you remember what I wrote about Joshik in Chapter 5, that breath control is a wonderful way to discharge negative energy from the body? If you're in pain when you press a BHP, it means that stagnant energy is being released from that spot. It's important to discharge as much of that energy as possible, breathing it out through your mouth. When your healing deepens, you may find yourself yawning, tears coming from your eyes and mucus from your nose. Exhaling or yawning has the effect of cooling down your brain by discharging hot energy from inside it.

When healing, it doesn't help to resist pain. The more you resist the pain, the worse it becomes. It's important to just accept it. Accept it dispassionately, without emotion, discharging the painful energy through your mouth. Have gratitude for being able to find and release the pain. And trust your body's natural healing ability. Tell yourself, "I'm not the one doing the natural healing. I merely trigger the natural healing; the rest I entrust to the power of life within me, believing that it will do what's best." Then you'll experience autonomous healing as your hands precisely locate and press BHPs, adjusting the intensity appropriately.

Without concentrating only on the pain while you press your BHP, let that pain be your guide, taking you deeper within. Try to watch and accept the state of your body and mind just as it is. That you have pain means that a lot of your energy is blocked and not circulating well. "I didn't realize this pain was inside me," you may think. "I've been under a lot of stress. I haven't taken good care of myself." Healing begins with self-watching and self-acceptance, feeling the condition of your body and mind just as they are. Without this process, there is no genuine change or healing, merely superficial and temporary fixes. The problems will seem to be resolved, only to return in full force later.

BHP Energy Healing is accompanied by emotional and spiritual changes as well as physical and energetic changes. Just as memories and emotions are stored in each organ and cell of our bodies, so, too, that kind of information is stored in our BHPs. Although we can't touch our organs directly, we *can* directly touch our BHPs. When you find specific spots where the flow of energy is blocked, you can work on them in a concentrated way. After doing that for a while, you'll experience emotional and spiritual blockages as well as physical ones being resolved and relieved.

For example, when you press your BHP, a certain memory that you rarely think of may suddenly come to mind as you realize that it is the root cause of some problem you're currently facing. The disorganized tangle of memories and thoughts in your head comes into clearer focus, and you may even find yourself shedding tears or forgiving someone as the emotions you'd suppressed are cleansed away. This is the process of Step 3 of Brain Education, Brain Refreshing, in which you release the emotional energy that has accumulated in your body and brain.

If you have several BHPs, heal them one by one. After you've pressed your BHPs enough, rest your hands on your knees, palms facing up. Close your eyes and breathe naturally. Bring to mind what the condition of your body was before you did the healing. Then try to let your brain follow up on the changes that occurred through the healing practice. Did your breathing become deeper and more comfortable? Did you feel your body growing lighter, your mind calmer? Did your body seem to be growing warmer and more comfortable overall, saliva collecting in your mouth and your eyes no longer feeling dry?

If you are especially sensitive to energy, you may detect various energy phenomena in your body. For example, after the energy blockages in your head open up, you may get a refreshing feeling in your head, as if you're showering in cool water. Or your entire brain may feel refreshed, as if you are holding a mint in your mouth. Occasionally, you might feel so much heat in your body that you break into a sweat, as if hot energy is circulating in your back and abdomen, and even in your hands and feet. This heat is proof that energy and blood are circulating vigorously throughout your body. Another energy phenomenon is the feeling that the whole body is more fluid, something that happens when your body has become an energy body.

Give your brain plenty of time to detect and enjoy the energy phenomena arising in your body. Let your brain be happy and proud of recovering balance and harmony. The happiness your brain feels will spread, bringing a smile to your face. This is an ideal state, in which the process of connecting with your body and transforming into an energy body has been wonderfully achieved. Try to maintain this feeling as you begin Pineal Gland Meditation, Step 4 of Brain Education, Brain Integrating.

Focus your awareness on your pineal gland. Even with your

eyes closed, you will feel as though you are inside a brilliant, dazzling light. The inside of your brain becomes bright, and you can see a light before your eyes. When the energy points on top of your head are opened through BHP Healing, you'll have the sensation of bright energy pouring down into your head.

Keep receiving that bright, refreshing energy of light pouring into your head and into your whole body. You may feel as if you're showering in light. You may also feel a liquid—like oil or honey, the water of life—flowing down from your head into your face and chest, and into your dahnjon, your lower abdomen. Then bundles of emotion that have been blocking your chest, feelings such as loneliness, resentment, anger, and sadness, may melt away. Simply entrust yourself to the flow of energy as heaven descends upon you. A numinous energy flows down into your body. Open yourself and connect with heaven.

"I've been blocking the energy of heaven," or, "I haven't been able to connect with heaven," you may realize as a deep awakening takes place within you. Continue accepting the energy of heaven and let it fill your dahnjon. You will feel energy flowing like the river of life, filling your lower abdomen like an ocean of energy as you become stabilized and fully centered in your core. And you reach a state free of all thoughts and ideas, in which extraneous thoughts and emotions have ceased—a state of muah in which your ego is gone. Your brain recovers a state of peace and equilibrium. That state is Step 4 of Brain Education, Brain Integrating, in which energetic integration and conscious integration have taken place. When this has been achieved and you are truly connected with yourself, a life of Brain Mastery begins.

Robert Puerto, an accountant in New York City, tells how BHP Energy Healing has helped him with physical healing:

I have been doing BHP Energy Healing now for over a month.

The healing has reminded me that I have the innate ability to heal my own body. It has taught me many energy healing points. I am looking forward to discovering other healing points, using my intuition.

With BHP Energy Healing, I could feel energy circulation in my body very strongly, and it would last the entire day. In the case of my kidneys, there have been times when I used to wake up three or four times in the middle of the night to use the bathroom, and in some cases almost every hour. Now I am only getting up one or two times on average, and I am getting more restful sleep.

One of the most important lessons I learned from the healing is to listen to my inner voice, my soul's voice. That voice is always talking. I just need to quiet my mind and listen. That voice tells me where healing is needed in my body. That voice always sends me love and compassion.

Renata Petryliene, who lives in Dallas, Texas, has experienced a real difference in her body and mind since she began BHP Energy Healing.

Since I started BHP Energy Healing four months ago, I have had tremendous changes in my body and mind. I have suffered from ciguatera fish poisoning, Lyme disease, Mast Cell Activation Syndrome, a stroke, gangrenous appendicitis, a brain aneurysm that gives me chronic fatigue, muscle and joint pain, high blood pressure, indigestion, and inflammation. There were days when I could not even get out of bed. My brain would be so clouded with negative thoughts that it was hard for me to focus, and I lost all self-confidence and hope.

From doing BHP Energy Healing one to five times a day, I have experienced relief from my pain, bloating, and fluid retention. My muscle and joint inflammation started to go down, my indigestion symptoms harmonized, and I began to get into the routine of training my body and mind. I used to have to take blood pressure medication every day, but now I only take it when it's needed. I even lost 10 pounds! My brain and mindset are clearer, I feel positive and calm inside even when there is stress, and I am able to fall asleep more easily and experience quality sleep for better recovery.

As mentioned in the testimonials above, BHP Energy Healing is particularly helpful for getting a good night's sleep. One factor that prevents restful sleep is a buildup of excess fire energy caused by too many thoughts milling about in the head. Opening up the blocked energy points in the head with stimulation makes it surprisingly easy for the brain to cool down. If possible, before you go to bed, quickly stimulate various points on your head for about five seconds each. Keep breathing out through your mouth as you expel the fire energy from your head. When your brain is worn out from excessive activity during normal times, this speedy BHP Energy Healing method can be used to quickly release fire energy. It is a sure-fire, amazingly effective way to reboot your brain. Even during the day, when your concentration is dropping or when you're tired or stressed, this can be a huge help in refreshing your brain.

I'll share with you the stories of people who have been experiencing purification and healing of their emotional energy through BHP Energy Healing. First is the account of a 68-year-old Korean woman named Wonhee Lim.

Under severe stress due to family relationships 20 years ago, I couldn't cry even when my husband died, and I couldn't cry afterward either, even when I was sad. As I practiced BHP Energy Healing, though, I found myself bursting into tears for the first time in 20 years. And in my heart I was able to forgive my husband. I'm so happy now that I can freely express both joy and sorrow.

Another story is that of a 51-year-old Korean construction engineer, Changhwan Bu.

For two years now, I've been suffering from a problem in my central nervous system, resulting in physical stiffness and a speech disorder. I received treatment in the hospital, but beginning about a year ago I didn't know what I was saying even while I was saying it, and my body was so stiff that everyday life was difficult. I learned about BHP Energy Healing three months ago and have been doing it every day. One day while I was doing the healing practice, I suddenly found myself laughing out loud. Since getting sick, I had never laughed out loud like that even a single time. After laughing to my heart's content, I felt my fears and worries vanishing and my confidence growing. I've been practicing BHP Energy Healing ever since. The headaches that were always troubling me have now disappeared, and I have hope for life. I often hear people around me saying that I look more cheerful than before.

This world is full of absolute life force, bringing balance and harmony to all things in creation. BHP Energy Healing restores your connection with this great life force. When that connection is restored, your life returns to its natural state of health and balance. Not only will you become physically healthier, but you'll recover your essence, natural and pure. Your good character and right judgment for serving and healing all things will revive as well.

When awakened through BHP Energy Healing and Pineal Gland Meditation, our brains search for ways to keep us in top condition—physically, emotionally, and spiritually. When the brain accurately detects a problem, it enters problem-solving mode. As our brains and bodies communicate with each other, they move as they need to, secreting hormones, causing stagnant energy to flow again, and creating powerful physiological and neurological changes. "Miraculous" stories of healing are born of this process. But when you understand the principles involved, you realize that these are not miracles at all, but a restoration of the senses and functions that are always latent in our bodies and brains. What's crucial in order for this to happen is connection. How closely is your brain connected with your body-mind? The stronger the connection, the more effectively and creatively the brain will work.

Our brains are not just decorations we carry around on our heads. They are supercomputers, gifts of the Creator that we should actively use. Check how well-connected your brain is with your body-mind. Through this connection, the power of life will awaken within you, bringing balance and harmony, and the healthier, more authentic life you will be able to lead.

You have the power to change your life. Wake up and develop that power by using Pineal Gland Meditation and BHP Energy Healing. You have the ability to increase your own natural healing power and change your life in positive ways, not leaving it all in the hands of others or relying on them for your health and quality of life. My earnest wish is for you to experience the infinite power of your brain through this simple but powerful technique of BHP Energy Healing, and for you to teach it to your family and friends. By doing so you will be helping many people lead healthier, more authentic lives.

CHAPTER 12

The Way to Light Up Your Consciousness Instantly

When people think of the brain, they generally think of it as an organ contained within the skull. It's an enigma, a soft and squishy blob that's responsible for processing all the complex information of the human mind. It's a universe in its own right, a frontier that modern science and medicine have yet to thoroughly investigate. Perhaps because people think neuroscience is too complicated to grasp and there isn't much they can do about their own brain, they don't seem to care all that much about it.

To properly use the power of the brain, we need a different attitude. The brain must not be viewed simply as another organ, like the heart or the lungs. Brain Education isn't about studying the number of neurons in the brain, the role of each area of the brain, or anything else about the brain's mechanical functioning. The focus instead is on unleashing the latent power of the brain and using it well in everyday life. For this, you have to start with "feeling" your brain—Brain Sensitizing. Rather than only seeing the brain as a physiological or anatomical organ, try to see it as the essence of your being. The brain is, indeed, the holistic expression of your physical, mental, and spiritual essence. Without your brain, you couldn't eat or love or do anything at all. Even when we feel our soul and divinity, all of that happens through the brain. Your brain is everything that has to do with you, as well as the *one* channel through which you connect and communicate with all of the external world—people, planet, universe. Being connected with your brain means meeting who you really are, and it means being connected with the true essence of the universe.

A different word to express the brain could be "consciousness." Because the brain exists, consciousness exists and functions. The function of consciousness can be divided into two classifications. The first consists of unintentional things that ordinarily happen automatically, even without our awareness of the brain's existence—like cognition, judgment, calculation, study, and memory. The second category is intentional consciousness. It's about doing things while consciously being aware of your brain. This is what Brain Education is more interested in.

Be aware of your brain right now, at this very moment. You'll feel your awareness filling up the inside of your brain. It's as if a light bulb in your brain has lit up, and that's how the light of your consciousness comes on. When that light turns on, you become the master of your brain. You become able to create the bright consciousness you want. "Brain = consciousness"—profound truth and enlightenment are hidden within these words. Brain Education is about attaining that enlightenment.

I'll teach you the second method of Brain Education that you can use to instantly light up the consciousness in your brain. It is a method for immediately checking the state of your brain, one that allows you to easily enter Brain Mastering mode. This is called Heaven's Gate Meditation, because it involves concentrating on Heaven's Gate, or *Chunmun* in Korean, in the crown of your head. You can instantly restore your brain's state of equilibrium through this meditation; it's especially helpful to take back your brain when you're in a Dark Brain state with your brain stuck in an undesirable state.

If you use the BHP Energy Healing that you learned in Chapter 11 to open up the energy points around your head before you begin this meditation, you can pass through Steps 1, 2, and 3 of Brain Education, and the effect will be doubled. By awakening the brain nerves with the right amount of stimulation, your brain is sensitized; by releasing stress and tension from the areas that were blocked, your brain becomes more versatile; and by releasing emotional energy along with pain, your brain is refreshed.

Heaven's Gate Meditation involves placing a small object, such as a rock, on the crown of your head and then practicing meditation. In general, when you're meditating well, random thoughts and emotions disappear, and you're able to focus on your body and your inner self. Placing an object on your head helps you to focus on that one thing, making it easy to break away from random thoughts and emotions. Your concentration is instantly maximized, and you focus fully within yourself.

Heaven's Gate Meditation

First you need to find a heavy-feeling stone, flat at the bottom. One that's too large could hurt you if it drops, so pick a rock that's about the size of a kid's fist. A book or other object that feels heavy and won't break will also work. Or you can use the five golden rings I developed specifically for this meditation. With five sizes and weights, they help you feel the gradual changes of energy as you use each ring one by one.

Sit in a chair or on the floor and straighten your back. Place the rock on your Heaven's Gate point at the top of your head. Rest your hands comfortably on your knees. Maintaining this posture, close your eyes and concentrate on your brain and body.

What sensations do you feel? The instant you place the stone on your Heaven's Gate, your brain will feel alert. All your senses and nerves will focus to keep the rock from dropping; your brain is that sensitive and agile.

Is it absolutely necessary to place the rock on top of your head, when you could just as easily put it in the palm of your hand or on some other part of your body? That's where the secret of Heaven's Gate Meditation lies. Even if you only consider physical structure, it makes sense. Since palms are flat with a dip in the center to hold things, there's little concern that a stone would fall off, so it's only natural that it would require less concentration. But if you place the stone on your head, which has a slightly rounded shape, even a small disruption in focus could cause it to fall, so it demands heightened focus. Also, if you place a stone atop the crown of the head, along the central line of the body, your body starts to balance itself. The spine and head are set straight, and the body's balance and angles are corrected. Furthermore, because the crown and brain are directly connected, your brain is stimulated the instant you place the stone on top of it, triggering various changes. The Heaven's Gate is a very important energy point that is located at the highest point of the body. When you place a stone on it, your awareness becomes focused there, your Heaven's Gate begins to open, and you begin to feel the clear, sacred energy of heaven entering your brain and body.

Feel the weight of the stone on top of your head. Weight is a form of energy. Feel that sense of weight come down through your head, through your chest, all the way down into your lower abdomen. An energy line is formed from your Heaven's Gate to your lower abdomen, and when it becomes stronger it will feel like a pillar of energy.

Slowly turn your palms upward and lift them about three inches from your knees. Straighten your spine and focus on your breathing. Feel your attention—previously focused outward or on your thoughts—gradually coming into your body. Feel your mind growing calm, your mouth filling with saliva, your breathing becoming deeper. Feel heavenly energy coming down from your Heaven's Gate like grains of sand falling in an hourglass, like the warm water of life flowing down into your whole body. Try to feel your brain. Isn't it more peaceful now? That is its natural state. You had merely forgotten that feeling. Now it's time to recover it.

When you get the feeling that your sense for peace and equilibrium has been restored, take the rock from on top of your head and place it on the floor. With your eyes closed, breathe as you concentrate on the feeling of your body, placing your hands on your knees.

Try to feel how you have changed, comparing your present state with how you felt before you did Heaven's Gate Meditation. Do your body and mind feel centered, and is your energy grounded? You may feel a heavy energy in the crown of your head, even though the stone is no longer there, and you may feel a thick pillar of energy coming down through your Heaven's Gate to your dahnjon in your lower abdomen. You may even feel the energy that is coming in through your Heaven's Gate descending along that pillar, gradually building up in your dahnjon. When your head is clear and refreshed, your lower abdomen is warm, and you feel grounded and centered, you've achieved the ideal state of balanced energy in your body that allows for a deeper level of Pineal Gland Meditation.

Again, visualize bright, luminous energy pouring down from heaven to your crown and to your whole body. Imagine a shower of light transforming every cell of your body, from the top of your head all the way to the tips of your fingers and toes. Your body transforms into bright light. You are inside this bright, radiant light. This is a state of being free from all thoughts and emotions, a state in which your ego has disappeared, a state of muah.

Try feeling your consciousness right now. You'll likely sense that a certain consciousness is looking down upon you from the back of your head. Can you feel that? That consciousness gazes down at you like an eye, crossing the boundaries inside and outside of you to calmly watch over everything about you. When you feel that, you will know with certainty that the eye of the pineal gland is open. It has merged as one with the divine cosmic consciousness. This is the purpose and meaning of Pineal Gland Meditation; this is also Brain Integrating, the fourth step of Brain Education.

The *Chun Bu Kyung*, the ancient text of Korea, begins with

One and ends with One, that "One" referring to the consciousness of One:

"Everything begins in One,
but that One is without beginning.
Everything ends in One,
but that One is without end."

This means that the world of consciousness is what has no
beginning or end. Meeting with that world is the absolute value
we are looking for. This is not something you can do by just
believing in it or that someone can do for you. The world of
consciousness can only be sensed for yourself when you awaken
the divinity dormant in your brain.

When your Divine Brain awakens, the eye of consciousness
opens. Then, you will be able to see. The hazy fog that was
clouding your vision will be cleared away, revealing the present
reality without distortion or delusion. There's nothing else to
enlightenment. It's simply being able to see the present reality
as it actually is.

Then, you will be able to hear. Your brain will let you hear
the optimal message that you most need. The moment you hear
that message, an "Aha!" will arise from within.

Then, you will be able to speak. The brain awakened inside
you will speak. You will express the message that you have seen
and heard. Through this, you'll be able to change your reality.

See, hear, and speak with the consciousness of the pineal
gland; this is Brain Mastery, the fifth step of Brain Education.

To become the master of your brain, connecting with and
feeling your brain is more important than anything else. That's
why I'm emphasizing that you must treat your brain as the embodiment of human character.

Put a smile on your face, and as you feel your brain, call to it by repeating several times, "My dear brain!" Don't you feel closer to it than when you just think of it as "brain"? Just as you grow closer to other people when you smile and call their names affectionately, you will be more closely connected with your brain when you call it "my dear brain." When your dear brain rejoices, it will produce positive hormones. Those hormones are the magic potion given to you by the Creator, a gift of love and blessings. Be grateful for the love you've received as you share it with people far and wide.

In Brain Education, you learn various ways to make the brain happy. Of course, meditation makes it happy, and music, action, messages, images, sound, and aromas can help as well. For example, if you play some upbeat music and dance freely with gleeful excitement in ways your dear brain wants, you'll feel the pulse of life in your heart as a smile blooms on your face from ear to ear. That's evidence that your dear brain is glad.

Once again, with your eyes closed and with your focus on your pineal gland, call out "my dear brain." Your brain will respond immediately. Try to feel this moment, right now. Sense your brain as it awakens to the here and now. That feeling is truth. Fully feeling the present means that your brain has awakened and recharged. The self created by your limited consciousness, the self created by the world, is just a story you and the world around you made up, a fiction. When can you escape from that illusion? Right now! A choice is possible only in the time we call "now."

You see a new world when you know the now. Take back your brain and awaken to the here and now. Open your Heaven's Gate and download the infinite energy and power of heaven. Creation and the phenomena of life occur moment by moment, in the here and now.

Utilizing the power of consciousness to change your condition or environment is the essence of using your brain. Become the master of your brain, the master of creation. This is possible because the seed of the Creator is there in your brain.

See, hear, and speak. Feel and actualize the infinite power in your brain. That is our calling, yours and mine—our noble, brilliantly shining mission.

I have been guiding people in Heaven's Gate Meditation in my recent workshops, many of them attended by Body & Brain Yoga practitioners. Here is the story of one of the participants, Michelle Parker, who lives in Scottsdale, Arizona. I hope that by reading her story you will gain further insight and motivation into this method of healing and awakening your divine consciousness.

From a very early age I have struggled with bipolar disorder that was difficult to manage. I was diligent in following the advice of medical doctors, psychiatric doctors, and counselors. I took handfuls of medication and eventually went through a series of transcranial magnetic therapy and ultimately 15 electric shock treatments, which left me frustrated physically, emotionally, and financially. Additionally, I started to develop migraines and was diagnosed with hypothyroidism and chronic kidney disease as side effects of the drugs. My family and my entire life were deeply affected in every way. But worst of all, I began to lose hope as I never quite found a balance between medications and treatments.

With so many mental and physical ailments, and a past career as a cardiac care unit nurse, I have always worked hard to "fix" or "get through" the toughest of times. I never gave up, yet I viewed my struggles as a chore in the most negative manner. In the past, my life centered around an illness to overcome. Looking back, I realize I also saw the world and its problems in the same manner—overwhelming and difficult to deal with, if not impossible.

I was fortunate to experience Heaven's Gate Meditation in a group retreat led by Ilchi Lee. He spoke passionately about loving yourself and connecting to the power we all have within. To wake up each day and speak to yourself. Speak to your brain as if it is the best friend that you have always had. I could feel my heart stir deeply when I sincerely told myself that I was doing a great job in this life. Speaking as he did, I was able to look at things differently. I found myself thanking my situation and struggles for the opportunity they have given me, and as I did this I could feel my soul awaken with hope and brightness and recognition.

The energy I experienced with Heaven's Gate Meditation was deliberate, warm, and healing and literally ignited the brightness of my spirit. I could feel my head become lighter and more open as I focused on the top of my head. I felt comfort knowing that this energy was coming down in such a loving manner with the intention of healing my body.

As the bright energy was descending upon me, my body began vibrating more and more deeply. My body movements were not directed by thought, and my awareness was that of an observer as I felt tension releasing and joints realigning. I could distinctly feel the warm, bright, and sincere energy swirling deeply into my bones and muscles and down to the very cells. Areas of blockages were losing their dark grip. I especially noticed the cleansing action in my right occipital lobe where I had physical and emotional trauma stored for such a long time. The dark sludge in my brain cascaded out as brilliant gems, giving me assurance that my brain was no longer impaired.

The brilliance was new, and I began to see how I could

truly use my past life experiences with mental illness in a healthy way to connect and help others heal from these same debilitating issues. I felt as if I was taking a tour of my inner body and was clearly aware of each nook and cranny as the vibrations and light deepened into my organs, almost as if I had been given a map to navigate. At one point I saw in my mind an X-ray view of my diseased kidneys being cleansed and healed and had the feeling that access to this healing energy was always around and within me.

The confidence and hope I felt was uplifting and empowering. I could feel my chest open and my heart and soul radiate with infinite love and assurance toward myself, and the boundaries between nature and mankind disappeared. At that moment it became very clear to me that as I give to myself, I give to others in the same manner. What a change from the depleted energy I had lived with before. Helping and healing others as I help and heal myself holds limitless possibilities!

Heaven's Gate Meditation opened my eyes to these things inside myself and to how my condition mirrors the world's condition. It gave me the gift of comfort in my own body, showed me the deep love that is always there inside my own heart, and most of all gave me hope.

PART IV

Stories of Transformation

CHAPTER 13

People Who've Found Solutions with Pineal Gland Meditation

Pineal Gland Meditation is a process of investigating the spiritual world, so at first glance you might think that it's not a practical exercise. But that's not actually the case. Pineal Gland Meditation is quite useful for everyday life because it enhances your problem-solving ability. Through it, you can leap beyond your limitations, finding solutions to your most pressing concerns.

"No problem can be solved," Albert Einstein once said, "from the same level of consciousness that created it." He was right. We must rise to a higher level of consciousness. Only then can we identify the cause of our problems and see how we should resolve them. You need "space" between the problems you're facing and your awareness in looking at them. Only with that freedom—looking at them from above, with a broader perspective—can you have real insight into your troubles. If you address your problems with the same consciousness that caused them, you will never be able to transcend the limited patterns of thinking that keep you trapped in that place.

Suppose there is a small box in front of you. The box is at eye level, so you only see one side of it and think that what you're looking at is the entire box. But if you look down from a higher, broader perspective, you'll see the other sides, too. In the same way, you can judge problems better from a higher, broader perspective, when you have some room to see things more clearly.

Let's say you had an argument with someone and were really hurt by what he said. "How could he do that?" you think, completely unable to understand his behavior. You end up feeling hate and resentment toward the other person, thinking everything is his fault. At this level of consciousness, you'd have trouble finding a way to solve the problem. You need to look at it from a higher perspective. Instead of pointing out other people's faults, seeing things only from your own perspective, you need to put yourself in the other person's shoes and look at the situation from his point of view. If you examine it objectively from a higher consciousness, you'll understand both sides, and you'll be able to find points of compromise.

Pineal Gland Meditation helps you create the space to look down at a problem from above, because meditation can brighten and elevate your consciousness. To rise to a higher consciousness, you must escape from thinking and feelings that are attached to the problem. Usually when some trouble develops, your thinking and feelings are completely wrapped around that issue. The cause of the problem is hidden by those thoughts and feelings. But if you focus entirely within yourself—breathing, and stopping your emotions through the Jigam, Joshik, and Geumchok steps of Pineal Gland Meditation—the essence of the problem will become distinct as the fog of your thoughts and emotions clears away. You will plainly see what had been hazy. And once you identify the cause of the problem, it will be easier to find a solution.

Through Pineal Gland Meditation, you can experience different powers being enhanced, powers that let you change yourself and your life. Physical, energetic, and spiritual healing take place. Your ability to regulate your emotions grows, as do your insight, intuition, foresight, judgment, tolerance, and creativity. If I had to name the most important of the powers heightened through Pineal Gland Meditation, I would choose these three: insight, creativity, and the drive and ability to get things done. Your problem-solving ability is enhanced when these powers act in an integrated way.

Insight comes from enlightenment. The first enlightenment is discovering and connecting with your true self. When you do this sincerely, you can start understanding, embracing, and loving yourself. You start to see the things that once concealed your true self. You see your character and habits, your patterns of thought and behavior, and you gain the ability to embrace your shortcomings, your limitations, and even your pain. And to the extent that your understanding of yourself has grown, you are able to understand others as well. Once you develop insight, you are able to have a broad view, seeing things from other people's perspectives, not just your own.

The second enlightenment is the great realization that everything is interconnected as one, and the ability to feel this with your entire being. You'll find no answers if you see everything as separate, according to the usual understanding. If you deal with your problems out of an awareness that everything is connected, though, you'll start to see answers.

Let's look at personal relationships as an example. Think of someone you have a conflict with. It won't be easy to resolve that conflict if you think of yourself as separate from the other person. Try changing your thinking. The two of you aren't separate; you're one. Bring the other person to mind, remembering that our universe came from one source—that everything is interconnected and one in the unseen world of energy and consciousness. Hating that person is hating yourself. Don't you feel a sense of regret for having resented this person who is one with you?

But what should you do if there's someone you really don't like? The best solution is to look at that individual with full compassion, from the same higher view you can use to understand yourself. They, too, acted the way they did because they were trapped in narrow ideas and old habits. How difficult must it be for them? Try to have compassion for them. Then a remarkable thing will happen. Your dislike will shrivel up, compassion welling up in its place. Not that long ago, you resented this person and couldn't forgive them. But now, the moment you empathize with them, realizing that they are another you, your resentment starts to disappear and be replaced by compassion.

The attitude you have in dealing with people changes fundamentally when you have this sense of connection. The brighter and broader your consciousness, the greater your empathy for the pain and suffering of others. When you view things with this insight, once-unsolvable puzzles fall into place as you realize the principles of life and the world. This is because you have opened your spiritual eye to see fully, looking all around you, instead of viewing the world from only one perspective.

Here is the story of Emma (name has been changed) and how Pineal Gland Meditation helped her find insight and a solution to marital problems that had troubled her for over a decade.

In the early sixties, I worked as a researcher at a pharmaceutical company. I met my husband while I was studying overseas, and after we got married we had a happy life with our daughter—that is, until he was in his mid-40s. He has a really sociable and outgoing personality, and he started going out, and staying out all night, unusually frequently. I realized that there was another woman. This was an unimaginable shock.

When I expressed my anger, my husband started cheating on me openly and being verbally abusive to me. It was as if he had become a totally different person.

I spent most days crying. I raged against my husband, even pleaded with him, but in his heart he didn't come back to me. What's more, he cheated with many women, not just one. I thought about divorce, but because of our young daughter, I wanted to avoid that if at all possible. So we decided that we would live separately in one house. From the outside, it looked as if we were a family without any problems. I became a workaholic, obsessively clinging to my work and not caring what my husband did. Even if I saw him with another woman, I would think, "It's okay, I'll just think about me and my daughter." I lived this way for over 10 years, enduring the hurt.

Last fall my little sister, who lives in Dallas, came to me and told me that her husband had witnessed mine living with another woman. My husband traveled to Dallas three or four times a year because of his work, but I'd never thought that he might be living with another woman there.

To my little sister, I pretended to be composed. Inside, though, all the emotions I had been suppressing now exploded. My well-maintained composure broke, and anger, resentment, and remorse overwhelmed me like a ferocious storm. My daily life became too difficult, and I was afraid to deal with people. What troubled me more than anything was the great resentment I felt toward myself. I felt worthless, like garbage. I suddenly felt disgust and hatred for myself. It was as if someone was shouting in my ear, "You're worthless. The life you've been living has been an empty shell." My life, all my efforts, seemed to be leaking through my fingers—a sandcastle crushed by an ocean wave. I felt miserable and lethargic, wondering what there was to live for.

About that time, I started doing Pineal Gland Meditation at a Body & Brain Yoga center. Pineal Gland Meditation caused memories buried deep in my unconscious mind to rise to the surface, one by one—not only happy ones, but painful memories and shameful experiences I didn't want to think about, and memories I didn't even know I had. But surprisingly, those memories showed me clear reasons and solutions for the physical, mental, and emotional problems I was experiencing. The instant I saw them, like puzzle pieces falling into place, I was able to understand—"Aha!"

I saw an image of myself bound tightly by a cord, unable to budge. At first I felt that cord was my husband, his cheating, and my environment—circumstances beyond my control. Looking deeper, though, I realized that the cord was actually the self I had believed was who I was. My ego, my habits, the education I'd received, and my fixed ideas were squeezing me so tightly that I couldn't breathe. After truly seeing myself and acknowledging this, that cord started falling away.

Then I was able to see my true self. "My substance is a precious jewel," I felt, warm tears flowing from my eyes. "I didn't see it because it was covered in filth. I've been living without knowing my true value." I saw myself feeling worthless and unimportant because my husband had betrayed me and no longer loved me. He had abandoned me, but I was the one who had abandoned my true self. Unable to let go of my attachment to my husband, I'd been living emotionally exhausted for a long time, going through the same pain again and again. I thought, "If I can't find myself, I'll live out my days in suffering, really amounting to nothing at all!" This realization hit me like a lightning bolt. And I promised myself, over and over, that I would consider myself precious, and that I would live for the growth of my soul. A shout burst out of my heart—"I am *who I am." Asking myself for forgiveness and expressing my gratitude, I told myself "I love you" so often that I was able to find reconciliation with myself.*

After encountering myself this way, I experienced changes greater than I could possibly have imagined. I ended up forgiving my husband. "My husband is also a precious jewel, like me," I told myself, beginning to understand him. "Living in the world, he gets dirty, bound by his limitations, which is why he behaved that way toward me." The suffering he had caused me was really painful, but I had found my true value through that experience, so I felt gratitude even for those difficult times. I felt compassion for him, struggling in a difficult reality, a man who had limitations, inadequacies, and hurts—just as I did. And I developed a sincere hope that he would learn how precious he is, and discover his own true worth. Realizing that the solution is ultimately found in the "self," the angry emotions that I had built up toward my husband disappeared like melting snow.

As I developed an inner center, at some point I was no longer troubled by the problems with my husband, and no longer critical of him. Before, I had agonized about whether I should divorce him; that no longer felt important to me. I completely let go of my attachment to my husband, for I realized that my value is not determined by his affection for me. What's important now is discovering my authentic self and asking what I want to do with the rest of my life. My fear and worry have changed to courage and confidence. Escaping from excuses and victim consciousness, I've decided to recognize my mistakes and take another step forward, boldly and confidently. It was as if I had struggled my way out of a long storm. Ultimately, I live my own life and live with my own choices.

Before, I didn't have the mental capacity to look after other people, since my head was all in knots over my own problems.

As I did Pineal Gland Meditation, though, I became interested in others, too, and developed a desire to help them. Now I've realized how precious are the connections among all of us, we who are living together in these times. My connections with my parents, brothers and sisters, daughter, relatives, friends, and colleagues, with all the communities to which I belong, and with the Earth itself—all feel precious and important.

One day I was meditating when my cousin came to mind, a mother dejected over having lost her son. Since she lived nearby, I went to see her and suggested that we go to a park together to exercise and get some fresh air. From this beginning, our numbers have grown one or two people at a time until now 10 of us go to the park twice a week for yoga and meditation. Everyone likes it, saying it brings vitality to their lives. The time spent meeting with them lets me catch my breath. No matter how busy all of us are, when it's time for our get-together we set aside whatever we're doing and go to the park to exercise and talk about life. It really opens our hearts, and we feel ourselves overflowing with the joy of living, of all of us being in this together.

Now I do with a joyful heart a lot of the tasks that used to feel hard, including my responsibilities at work. I want to grow and develop my abilities so that I can help others more, even if only a little. I'm thankful for the realization that all the difficulties I encounter in life are opportunities for growth. I'll live this life that I've chosen, never fearing or giving up, because I know my true value. I feel a real peace inside now, one that fills my heart, not the fake peace I used to pretend for the sake of appearances.

Emma's testimony vividly shows the power of Pineal Gland Meditation. When we dig really deep into the fundamental causes of our suffering, we find that they haven't been external factors at all. They have come about because we've been disconnected from ourselves. We are able to see that we have been trembling with fear, concerned about what others think, without knowing who we really are or what our true value is. The moment we realize this, we discover new value—an absolute, internal value, not a relative, external one. And when we discover that value, we develop a clear center. That center is the power of the soul, manifesting itself when we connect with our true self. The power of the soul is love and tolerance.

Pineal Gland Meditation, at its core, is about practicing loving yourself. This is unquestionably tied in with loving others. Consider the following:

- Failing to understand others means failing to understand yourself. You can understand others to the extent that you understand yourself.

- You can embrace others to the extent that you embrace yourself. Failing to embrace others means failing to embrace yourself.

- Failing to love others means failing to love yourself. You can love others to the extent that you love yourself.

- Resenting others means resenting yourself. You won't resent others to the extent that you don't resent yourself.

- Being attached to things or other people to validate your worth shows how empty you are inside. You will feel fulfilled to the extent that you have inner fullness.

You can also love the world to the extent that you love yourself. Loving the world while not loving yourself, from a certain point of view, is hypocrisy. You will eventually burn out if you try to extract from yourself something you lack. But when you truly love yourself, the energy of the love inside you automatically emerges and flows out into the world.

All people live their lives pursuing their own interests. They want to do what they like, not what they don't like. That's called selfishness, but selfishness isn't always a bad thing. People always think in ways that are centered on themselves; that's unavoidable because it's simply how we all experience the world. What's more important is how far that "self" extends. There will be forms of selfishness that consider only the small self of the ego, and forms of selfishness that think of the big self, connected and one with all things. If you think of the big self as "me," then the selfishness that seeks to benefit that self will naturally be altruistic. When you have no sense of separation between yourself, other people, and the world, then loving yourself is loving the world, and loving the world is loving yourself. You realize this automatically when you develop insight into oneness through Pineal Gland Meditation. The power of pure, unconditional love emerges based on that insight.

Creativity is another significant power enhanced through Pineal Gland Meditation. When your pineal gland is activated, creative ideas will come to mind, ideas you'd never thought of before. Have you ever focused intently on something when suddenly an original idea came to you? Where do such ideas come from?

When you do Pineal Gland Meditation for a while, you'll get the feeling that your brain is connecting to the cosmic brain, accessing the database of the universe. While we sleep, our brains process unconscious information and data from the day's experiences; our dreams are said to be one form of such activity. Could it be that while our thinking brain and emotional brain are relaxed, we're accessing the cosmic brain in our sleep, uploading our personal information and downloading cosmic information?

This communication of information happens automatically while we sleep. But there is also a way to access the cosmic brain when we are awake—through Pineal Gland Meditation. During sleep, our brain waves are generally in a theta or delta state; through meditation we can create those same brain-wave states. We can enter the world of the unconscious, accessing the cosmic brain and downloading cosmic information while we are awake, just as we do while we sleep. This involves bringing to mind any issues you're worried about while your pineal gland is activated through Pineal Gland Meditation.

I describe this by saying, "Ask your brain." Then your brain goes to work, searching for an answer to your question. At some point it tells you the answer. You may see this as an image or hear it as a message. This isn't your thinking brain or emotional brain, not a state of consciousness built up by random thoughts and emotions. It's a world of integrated awareness, accessible when you've entered your deep internal consciousness. It's a state of muah, a state at which the forth step of Brain Education, Brain Integrating, has been attained. The pineal gland is a channel through which your brain accesses the cosmic brain. But you can find real answers only if you ask your brain when that channel is turned on and operating.

Lynn, a practitioner of Pineal Gland Meditation, describes her own experience of creative empowerment.

I was put in charge of a big new project at work. But I thought that there was no way I could handle this assignment, given my current skills, so it felt like a huge burden to me. I'm not good enough at this or that, I thought, so will I really be able to take this on? Wouldn't it be okay to not do it? I drew boundary lines around my skills in this way, feeling uncomfortable because of the weight of this project. I mean, it was so bad that I couldn't really sleep at night, and I even lost my appetite. After several days of that, I was deeply immersed in Pineal Gland Meditation one day when I brought this worry to mind and asked what I should do. A remarkable thing happened right away. It was like an incredibly loud voice exploding in my pineal gland, saying, "I can do it!"

It was astonishing how loudly the message rang through my head, echoing not once but repeatedly. The voice was so loud that I wanted to shout, letting it out through my mouth. I couldn't do that, though, since there were people quietly meditating around me. I formed my hands into fists, squeezing them tightly to keep from screaming, and immense tension went through my arms and legs, my abdomen and lower back—my whole body. My muscles flexed and my arms shook, and my body grew hot, dripping with sweat. The stronger the tension in my body became, the louder the message—"I can do it!" It boomed in my pineal gland and seemed to be imprinted on every cell of my body.

My attitude totally changed after that. "Okay, let's see who wins, you or me," I said to the work facing me, rolling up my sleeves and diving headfirst into the assignment. As I tackled the work, original ideas popped up in my brain, one after another. I worked with incredible power and concentration, with the result that the project was a great success. I had created a small miracle, successfully completing a job that some had thought impossible.

After receiving a powerful message from my pineal gland, my brain had put itself completely into project mode. Whether I was sitting or standing, eating or going to bed, my brain was totally filled with thoughts about the project. It felt as if my brain was charged with powerful energy. I was filled with confidence, and new ideas kept coming to me. I realized that I was

no longer restricted by what I had considered my limitations.
Those limitations were merely illusions I had created.

When your pineal gland is activated and connects with the cosmic brain, you can see reality clearly. The things you thought were limitations—barriers you were afraid to challenge—are a matrix of sorts, created by your own fixed ideas and preconceptions. You could break through these seemingly impenetrable walls at any time if you truly wanted to. It's all up to you. Pineal Gland Meditation fundamentally changes the mind, the consciousness. The most powerful strength—creating being out of nothingness—is found in the mind and nowhere else. In the case of Lynn, even after she received a message through Pineal Gland Meditation—"I can do it!"—her environment was the same as it had been before. If anything had changed, it was this: her mindset. Her change of mind was a driving, creative force, transforming her external environment and making possible what had once seemed impossible.

When you look for solutions to your problems through Pineal Gland Meditation, one important element is concentration. You could say that Lynn's concentration shook her pineal gland awake as she focused on that project so intently. To do this for yourself, live your daily life as you always have, but in your subconscious awareness, never let go of your thoughts about any problem you consider important. Don't worry about them, but instead just hold them close to your heart. Like a brooding hen sitting on its eggs, calmly incubate the issue in the back of your mind. Then your brain will start to search your unconscious information, the cosmic database, to find a solution. At some point, a truly creative idea will come up.

Access to the cosmic brain doesn't happen only when you're meditating with your eyes closed. If you maintain your focus, ideas will suddenly come to you even in your daily life. They will pop into your head when you're reading, when you're showering, when you're brushing your teeth, when you're cleaning, when you're doing the dishes, when you're exercising, when you're out for a walk, when you lie down to go to sleep, when you open your eyes in the morning, when you have conversations with other people. Sometimes more creative ideas will come to you while you're going about trivial tasks than when you're sitting at a desk pondering over an issue. When you've been holding problems in the background of your mind and then suddenly enter a state free of thoughts and emotions, the information of the universe becomes downloaded into you with a click.

If you get a clear message through Pineal Gland Meditation, you also receive the power to act on it—for that message is powerful, coming from the world of integrated consciousness and not from mere thoughts. This is the third important power enhanced through Pineal Gland Meditation: the drive and ability to get things done. It's the power to act in an innovative way. A completely new power is manifested, one you had been unaware of before and not a repetition of existing behavior patterns. The source of that power is *clarity*. The buzz of other distracting thoughts is quieted because the message arising from your consciousness when you are in a state of deep meditation is so clear. A fire is lit in your heart, enhancing your drive to achieve that one goal. Then you are able to use this new power instead of the restricted power you had before, trapped in your limitations. You are able to attract and use the power and energy of the cosmos as you are connected with the cosmic brain through the channel of your pineal gland.

Let me introduce someone who found that even weight control was made possible, along with other important life changes, through the enhanced drive and power to get things done that she received with Pineal Gland Meditation. Bama Kim is one of the New York regional managers of Body & Brain Yoga. The following is her testimony.

I attended Ilchi Lee's lecture at a retreat in Sedona, Arizona, in the summer of 2017. That was when I first came across his ideas about a 120-year life. It felt preposterous at first, but I was attracted by the audacious thought that I could be more intentional about my lifespan, and his message that I could design the rest of my life from a long-term perspective really hit home. So I asked myself, "Do you think you can make it to be 120 living the way you do now?" Immediately I thought, "No way." That question brought many others, falling like dominoes. I was 45 years old, at the midpoint of my life, a time when I needed to check how I'd been doing.

About that time, I finally started practicing Pineal Gland Meditation seriously almost every day. What I feel the most when I do Pineal Gland Meditation is that I really become more tranquil. And my spine stands up straight. When I do sitting meditation for a long time, my back often slumps or gets tired. With Pineal Gland Meditation, though, I've never had that feeling. My mind grows more tranquil, my body straighter, and the thought that I should change and want to change becomes very clear. So I asked myself during Pineal Gland Meditation, "What should I change?" That's when a message came to mind that I should get up early in the morning. I had always wanted to start the day earlier, but I hated to give up my morning sleep and didn't want to cause myself stress, so I hadn't really been able to act on that desire.

During meditation, I made up my mind to get out of bed earlier, but I intentionally didn't set my alarm before going to bed. I wanted to see how I would react. Surprisingly, the next morning I woke up two hours earlier than normal! Before, I was getting up at around seven o'clock. But that day I woke at five o'clock—and I also got up early the next day, again without an alarm. The problem, I realized, was that I hadn't really resolved to do this before. My resolve hadn't been strong enough to engrave it in my unconscious mind as I had now done through Pineal Gland Meditation.

Since I was now waking up two hours earlier, it felt like I had twenty-six hours in the day. While doing Pineal Gland Meditation, I asked myself how I would use those extra two hours. It occurred to me that I should study human beings. As a trainer at Body & Brain Yoga, I help people recover health of body and mind, so I felt that understanding them more deeply would enable me to help them better.

I started researching the worries and problems people commonly have, reading books related to psychology or the humanities and searching for information online. For example, I focused on problems or concerns people may have when they can't properly express their emotions. I read books about this, listened to lectures, and talked about it with other people. I started directly applying the things I learned to my own life, as well as giving advice to people around me who needed it. I did this actively and passionately, and positive changes started happening both in my life and in the lives of others. The more I did this, the more fascinating and precious my two hours of morning study time felt. Since then, for over a year now, I've been applying in my life what I've learned by studying early in the morning.

Throughout this process, daily Pineal Gland Meditation has acted as a compass for me. When I look back over my tasks for the day through meditation in the evening, concentrating within myself, the subjects I need to study next naturally come to mind. For instance, if thoughts about acceptance come to mind while I do the meditation, I strive to practice acceptance in my daily life as I focus on studying that subject. Such times have given me an opportunity to really expand my understanding of human nature. Before, I often couldn't understand why people did the things they did. Now, though, I'm starting to understand. I'm judging others less, and I'm thinking more about how I can help them. Of course, I see my own problems better, too.

Maybe I should say that my interest in, understanding of, and compassion for people have deepened. My genuine interest in understanding humans better—including myself—and my desire to help them have intensified. This gives me more peace of mind and more freedom. Even when things haven't worked out as I'd like, I've been less anxious and worried and have had less trouble believing in myself. I haven't been as fearful about results. Through Pineal Gland Meditation, I clearly saw myself being sensitive to the assessments of others. I mean, I hadn't thought I was that way at all. When I looked at where that sensitivity came from, I found that it was from a fear of rejection—a fear of not being loved, of not being recognized, of feeling my value be decreased. My deeper understanding of myself enabled me to better help others who have the same problems.

The greatest physical change I experienced as I went through this process was losing weight. I lost 30 pounds in one year— even though I wasn't intentionally controlling my weight. What I ate didn't especially change, and I didn't exercise more enthusiastically than usual. But I gradually and naturally lost weight, losing a couple of pounds a week and then repeatedly hitting a plateau, only to lose more again later. This seems to *have been the result of having less stress. My interest in people continued, so I wasn't as irritable or stressed. Such emotions use an incredible amount of energy, and typically people try to make up for that by consuming more food. Since I lost about 30 pounds, the power in my body could have decreased, yet my vitality remained the same. The amount I ate decreased naturally. When people ask me my secret, I tell them these two things: getting up two hours earlier in the morning and taking a genuine interest in people.*

The changes I experienced over the last year started with a question: "Do you think you can make it to be 120 living the way you do now?" When I seriously asked myself that question, I had a kind of awakening in my pineal gland. For me, Pineal Gland Meditation is a time for reflecting on myself. When I looked at myself honestly, I felt what I should do and I just did it. Comparing myself now with who I was a year ago, I sense great change. I believe this is the result of implementing in my life the messages I received through regular Pineal Gland Meditation.

Pineal Gland Meditation elevates consciousness vertically. Through logical thinking or knowledge, consciousness merely shifts horizontally. If you are unable to make a great jump—getting better only to get worse again, continuously and repeatedly—then your consciousness is just shifting horizontally. You seem to change a little, only to end up going back to your old patterns of thought and behavior. Pineal Gland Meditation, however, makes possible a vertical elevation of consciousness. A jump in consciousness occurs when you encounter and connect with a completely new self, not the self you thought was you— your big self, not your little self.

Are you facing limitations or suffering because of some troubling problem? I hope you will consider this moment a great opportunity to experience a vertical elevation of consciousness. The pressure you feel right now, interpreted negatively, is great stress but interpreted positively, it's an increase in internal pressure that empowers a leap of consciousness. When you earnestly want to escape from your confusing and frustrating present circumstances, not knowing what you to do causes even more frustration. But if you press one powerful button, a massive explosion will happen inside you. In an instant you'll see everything clearly, as if a fog has been lifted. That button is the pineal gland in your brain.

CHAPTER 14

My Own Pineal Gland Story

I experienced an explosion of consciousness through Pineal Gland Meditation about 40 years ago, when I was 30. At the time I was a medical laboratory technologist, a husband, and the father of two children. On the outside, my life looked ordinary and uneventful, but, inside me an incredible fireball of anguish was burning away.

That anguish began when I was a child. My life was like a tree that had failed to put down roots. Things were very dark for me growing up, especially after being shocked by an incident when I was 14—the death of my friend. "Death" felt vividly real to me at that young age, and my mind roiled with all sorts of questions and images as a result. I would relentlessly ask myself, "Why do I live? What meaning does life have if I'm going to die anyway?" The harder I thought about it, the more everything seemed to come back to one conclusion: "I'm going to die anyway." This gradually changed me into a skeptic and a pessimist. Unable to see the meaning in life, I naturally had no interest in studying. Moreover, having a severe attention deficit disorder put up a wall between me and studying; at school I was a misfit, and for my parents I was disappointing as a son. I rarely thought about planning for a better future. I was just living however things worked out, since I couldn't find any meaning in life.

One day when I was wandering about, having failed the

college entrance exams twice, I saw a big pile of garbage underneath a bridge. I felt I was like that garbage—discarded, good for nothing, liked by no one. I felt as if I had no future, no hope. After many twists and turns, I did get into college, graduated, found a job, and started a family, but I wasn't happy. And an unidentifiable emptiness and sadness never left my heart. No matter what I did or whom I was with, that void was never filled. Living without knowing who I was, or why I was living at all, was painful. Other people all seemed to be fine, living their lives without any problems, so I couldn't understand why I alone was so troubled. I reached a point where I thought that unless I could resolve my anguish, I would no longer be able to endure it. The agony was so great, so troubling, that I couldn't focus on my life.

I decided to put everything else aside and take time to focus completely on myself. That's why I went to Mt. Moak, near Jeonju in South Korea, to begin an ascetic practice. I made up my mind to go without eating or sleeping until I found an answer I could truly feel satisfied with. And I asked just one question, over and over: "Who Am I?"

About three weeks passed, and I lost my sense of time. I didn't know whether it was day or night, and was having difficulty determining even whether I was awake or asleep. All I could feel was an extremely severe headache. I tried all kinds of crazy things to get rid of the pain in my head, even standing on my head, but the headache only got worse. Fear washed over me, a feeling that if I continued like this, my head might explode and I would die.

At some point I abandoned all effort to do anything about it. Completely setting aside any thought of resisting the pain, I sat down, closed my eyes, and controlled my breathing. And I just accepted everything as it was. Then I sensed a massive explosion in my head, along with what sounded to me like thunder.

Instantly I was so peaceful and tranquil, it was as if my head had disappeared. This sensation was so real that before I even realized what I was doing, I reached up to check whether my head was still there. I had the feeling that my body and all of the boundaries around me had vanished within a silence I had never before experienced. And the whole cosmos filled the place where I was, spreading out all around me.

Then a question rose up in my mind. "Who am I?"

I heard a response at the same time. "I am cosmic energy. I am cosmic mind."

That answer didn't come from my thoughts. It was a message echoing from the deepest place in my consciousness. That message filled me, and it had a clarity that put it beyond all doubt. I was truly cosmic energy and cosmic mind.

All boundaries between inside and outside disappeared. I felt that I was eternal life, existing alone within endless tranquility and peace. What had been born and would die was merely my body; my essence was eternal life itself—infinite, without beginning and without end. I was heaven and earth; there was not a thing in the world that was not me. Everything was One.

That was the world I saw. It was not the physical world, seen with physical eyes. It was the world of consciousness, the world of energy, seen with the eyes of consciousness—with the spiritual eye. This happened when my pineal gland was opened. The realization that I am cosmic energy and cosmic mind came to me as light, sound, and waves, perceived by my whole heart, my whole consciousness.

That experience on Mt. Moak completely changed everything in my life. For I had finally found the answer to the question that had been hounding me, stubbornly and painfully—who am I? My essence was cosmic energy and cosmic mind! After realizing that, my heart was filled with incredible joy. I had no reason to envy others, for I had finally realized who I really am. It seemed as if the whole world was mine.

My name, thoughts, knowledge, experience, and profession—these were not me. And my value wasn't determined by the evaluations of others. It had nothing at all to do with popularity, with the praise or criticism of the world. I was life itself, immeasurable, infinite, lacking nothing, whole and beautiful and great. That was my absolute value, my true self. The relative value assigned to me by my ideas, and those of others and the world—that wasn't me. I was moved so deeply, so filled with awe, that I felt the sublime within myself; I came to truly love myself. What moved me most deeply was that other people also have and can discover the exact same value and true self that I did. The great life I felt was not only my substance, but the substance of all people, of all things existing in the universe. All life, including mine, has its own unique, absolute value and beauty, being interconnected in one great life.

I came to embrace the dearest hope that when everyone awakens to the absolute value of the true self within them, all of society as well as the life of each individual will clearly change. However, a regret also grew along with that hope. There is a Korean saying about "for three years looking for your baby you're carrying on your back." This means that you do not know what is so close to you. I thought of people living their whole lives wandering as I had in search of themselves—selves that are so close but also somehow invisible to them. They scurried about, rotely doing the busy work of life, never knowing the amazing reality of their true self—cosmic energy and cosmic mind. Disease, I realized, is the state of being disconnected from the flow of cosmic energy, the wellspring of life that never dries up; the pain and mental conflict humans suffer is a result of being disconnected from the cosmic mind.

This realization brought me an earnest desire to help people reconnect with cosmic energy and cosmic mind—their true self. I resolved to share cosmic energy, helping people who suffer from disease, and share cosmic mind, healing people's wounded hearts and the world.

This is the oath I made to heaven, the purpose I engraved on my heart before coming down from Mt. Moak. It was only after I awoke to who I truly am and what I should live for that—to my great relief—I finally felt meaning in my life. Finally I had a definite reason for living. This reason made my heart pound. And this reason became my spirit.

Afterward, I identified the three powers of insight, creativity, and the drive and ability to get things done. These same three powers were illustrated in the stories told in the previous chapter about people who found solutions through Pineal Gland Meditation.

First, I developed insight. I saw why people are troubled and suffering, and I suddenly understood why the world works this way. While the process of my own seeking had been difficult and painful, the substance of enlightenment is actually within easy reach. The essence is to discover and live connected with your true self. Therefore, I decided to find ways to make enlightenment understandable and attainable, enabling anyone so resolved to follow the path easily.

My personal situation and the people around me didn't change just because I had awakened, however. I came down from Mt. Moak and saw that everything was just as it had been before. Only one thing had changed: my consciousness and my spirit. So first of all I decided to believe in myself. I felt that the only person I could trust was me. That's really how it was. Enlightenment wasn't written on my face, and it's not as if someone was going to support me because I had awakened. I had no alternative but to find ways for myself—to create and to act. This doesn't mean that some epic, eye-opening plan came to me. I just made up my mind to believe in myself and move as my soul felt I should, as my spirit guided me.

I got up early in the morning on the day after coming down from the mountain, and I went to a nearby park. There I met a stroke patient. I approached him and started up a conversation, wanting to help him somehow. I massaged his legs, since he lacked freedom of movement, and I taught him some simple exercises, adjusted to his physical condition. My only thought was, "I'll do it if it helps him even a little bit." I went to the park every day and showed him various exercises, and others started gathering around as well, one by one. They would stand watching and wondering, quizzical expressions on their faces, until they started following along, doing the movements I was teaching.

Folks kept coming together like this, the park echoing every morning with the sounds of people tapping their dahnjons and doing the exercises to a count—"One! Two! Three! Four!" There was the sound of laughter as they massaged each other's shoulders and patted each other's backs. Watching everyone, I was happy, too, and excited, a smile covering my face. Thinking about it now, that was the time of my life when my soul was happiest. I mean, having spent my youth sunk in self-recrimination, I was utterly amazed, unable to believe that I could now help someone, that I could make someone smile. It was a completely new me, a picture of myself that would have been totally unimaginable before. And even then, I had no idea that this would become a turning point, completely changing my life.

The class had begun in the summer, and it kept going into the fall and winter. When the weather got so cold that it was hard to continue, one of the participants made a proposal. There was space in his building, he said, suggesting that we hold classes there. I started leading classes indoors the next day, making it possible for me to teach a variety of exercises and meditative methods that used sitting or reclining postures.

While all that was going on, I did research and thought deeply about how I could more effectively share what I had experienced. During that process, I ended up studying the traditions of Sundo handed down in Korea since ancient times, discovering that my own experiences were consistent with the teachings of this system. So, restoring the ancient traditions of Sundo and combining them with a modern understanding of the human body and mind, I developed a system of theory and training methods. Five years later I ended up opening a small center, about 900 square feet in size. Since then it has spread out into the world as hundreds of Body & Brain Yoga and Brain Education centers. I established a university to develop Brain Education as an academic discipline, and I have written more than 40 books sharing my methods and experiences. I've traveled to many countries and regions, lecturing and meeting countless people.

This wasn't all planned out and prepared from the beginning. What made it possible was my personal conviction. I believed in myself. That self was the substance of who I am—cosmic energy and cosmic mind, realized through enlightenment, not the self of my thoughts and emotions. I always went back to myself whenever negative thoughts and feelings arose, or whenever people around me told me something was impossible. I would close my eyes and immerse myself in deep meditation, connecting with my true self. Then I'd see a way forward. I'd hear the messages of heaven, and new ideas would come to mind.

Whether 40 years ago or now, my day begins the same way. I get up in the early morning every day. My eyes open all on their own, and my brain wakes up by itself. Then I immediately sit down and close my eyes, and I focus on my pineal gland. When I do that, inspirational messages come to me, or I think of solutions to issues I had pondered about the previous day. Or the work I should do or the faces of people I should meet that day come to mind. Dawn is when my awareness is clearest. As the channel to my pineal gland opens, it feels as if my brain is accessing the cosmic brain, downloading cosmic information. I can confidently say that the things I've achieved so far are the result of messages I've received through my pineal gland at dawn every day. What's more, when I'm in nature, when I meet people, or when I give a lecture, I approach whatever I'm doing with the consciousness of insight, with my spiritual eye able to see beyond my physical eyes.

The path of my life hasn't exactly been a well-paved highway, broad and easily traveled. The obstacles I've broken through have been more numerous than I can count. It has been the misunderstandings and betrayals of people, not the obstacles of my physical environment, that have troubled me most. Often I've been indescribably lonely; frequently I've had to make major decisions alone, without being able to discuss them with anyone.

For example, I left my base of support in Korea when I was over 40 years old and crossed over to America, a strange land, to start over from the ground up. I took over a retreat center in the middle of the desert in Sedona, Arizona—a place that the previous American owner had been unable to operate successfully. Here I created Sedona Mago Retreat Center, a healing and training facility. Another challenging project for which I had to break through people's preconception and dissuasion was creating the Benjamin School for Character Education in South Korea, a school that lacks five things—classrooms, set curriculum, homework, tests, and grades. Now the school is successfully offering many students a chance to encounter their true self and discover their own value.

When I began all these endeavors, common sense made it glaringly obvious that I would fail. Everyone around me tried to dissuade me, saying, "No. That's impossible." That seemed apparent, looking at it only from the perspective of the visible world. But then I closed my eyes and focused within myself. And I connected with heaven—cosmic energy and cosmic mind—inside myself. Again and again, I asked myself whether I had within me the sincere longing to do that work, and whether that work was needed, whether it would really contribute to people and the world. When a feeling of certainty filled me, I made my decision. And then I never looked back. I pursued the work with great focus, creativity, and the drive and ability to act. What enabled me to continue attracting and using these powers was my daily Pineal Gland Meditation.

Pineal Gland Meditation has been the key to closing the gap between my dreams and reality. The dreams I have are not small, so turning them into reality is inevitably accompanied by difficulties. But whenever things are hard, whenever I run up against obstacles, whenever negative thoughts rush over me, I obtain new ideas and the power to push aside obstacles through Pineal Gland Meditation. Whenever I have a problem in reality, instead of looking with dread only at the problem, I've focused more on my pure longing for that dream to become reality. Through Pineal Gland Meditation, I've imagined my dream becoming real and have downloaded cosmic energy, comforting and encouraging myself amid my troubles and getting myself back on my feet.

Doing the meditation deeply, I feel a clear before-and-after difference. Before meditating, the power of reality dominates—being troubled, feeling like things won't work out, wanting to give up. But after doing Pineal Gland Meditation, my dream feels close, and I feel as if I can break through any obstacle. It's important to close the gap between dreams and reality through meditation in this way. When you feel certain you can do something, you will be able to tap into the power to achieve your dreams. Once you've connected with the source of that power—the source of insight, creativity, and the driving power to act—all you have to do is pull it out and use it. That's possible for anyone who has a body, brain, and consciousness. It's an app, a program—creativity and the operations of consciousness—that's already installed in human beings. All you need to do is make use of it.

The universe is filled with life, with cosmic energy and cosmic mind. That life is the energy and power leading and directing all living things. When we connect to this power and energy, they guide us in the direction we should go, like migrating birds instinctively flying home to breed or like salmon returning to the place of their birth to spawn. When we're connected with the source of life, we realize what it is we need. We feel a fundamental peace amid a sense of complete oneness, and we gain the power to create the lives we truly want.

I've felt great hope as I've watched the consciousness of more and more people awakening through Pineal Gland Meditation, seeing them beginning to use the power of creation to build a new future for themselves, people, and the world. Nothing is more joyful or moving than seeing people discover that they have the power to change the world as well as their own lives.

I'm grateful today, too, that I've been given another day of precious time. I'm thankful it allows me to contribute in a small way to the work of awakening the great human spirit, the true value of humanity that lives in all people.

CHAPTER 15

Connecting Heaven to Earth

Through Pineal Gland Meditation, we can experience a world of brilliant light, infinite love, and peace and oneness unimaginable within conventional consciousness. One thing we must guard against, though, is letting it end as nothing more than an amazing experience. Meditation would have little meaning if it amounted to no more than that. How would experiencing bright light and the world of energy through meditation be any different from watching a spectacular 3D fantasy movie?

Long ago, coming down the mountain after obtaining enlightenment, I engraved on my heart these words: "Enlightenment that cannot be shared is not true enlightenment." No matter how wonderful, mysterious, or spiritual the experiences I've had through meditation may be, if those experiences have no effect on reality, then they exist only at the level of thought.

I suggest you to reflect seriously on our ultimate purpose for doing Pineal Gland Meditation. We can find a hint in the very last sentence of the ancient Korean text, the *Sam Il Shin Go*:

"The enlightened one stops his feelings (Jigam),
controls his breathing (Joshik),
and prohibits contact (Geumchok),
going forward with only one purpose,

reflecting on delusion to arrive at truth,
finally spreading far and wide the energy of heaven;
that is achieving Sungtong Gongwahn."

The *Sam Il Shin Go* presents Sungtong Gongwahn as the ultimate goal of spiritual practice. *Sungtong* means awakening to your true nature and achieving unity with divinity, the true nature of the cosmos. *Gongwahn* means carrying out meritorious service, completing the work you should do for the world. If Sungtong refers to enlightenment and completion on an individual level, then Gongwahn refers to promoting the completion of the whole by spreading individual enlightenment in the world. Awakening to your true nature and completing your mission in the world, pursuing completion of the whole as well as your individual completion—here we find the clear purpose of Pineal Gland Meditation.

Stated more simply, we could call this "connecting with the greater self." The deeper the stage of Pineal Gland Meditation, the more we experience the "self" we perceive being gradually transformed, growing and expanding. Before you started Pineal Gland Meditation, you probably saw a false self as "me," one consisting of your thoughts, ideas, and emotions. Through Pineal Gland Meditation, you've learned how to separate the energy of your soul from the energy of your emotions and connect with your soul, as explained in Chapter 7. Through this process, you've realized that your true self is the energy of the pure soul in your heart.

And then your perception of yourself underwent another transformation. The energy of the soul in your heart longs to be connected with a greater world. As I shared in Chapter 8, when that energy of longing reaches the Heavenly Palace in your brain, your pineal gland is activated and you reconnect with your divinity. In this state, you experience cosmic consciousness, a world of integration and unity. You are immersed in a bright light with the energy of heaven coming down through Heaven's Gate. Then, a great transformation occurs in your perception of yourself, changing from the self of your soul to the self that is one with the cosmos. You experience an explosion of enlightenment in your brain—"I am the cosmos. All is one." Instantly all your questions and all the noise are swept away. That was my realization—"I am cosmic energy and cosmic mind"—and that is your true self.

The journey to find your true self begins by feeling the energy of your soul like a tiny seed in your heart. It is not all of what you are looking for, though. It is not the soul confined in your heart, but the soul that becomes one with divinity, cosmic consciousness, that is your ultimate identity, your true self. And once you awaken to this, your soul's energy continues to grow and evolve into a vast world by manifesting your awakening.

Then your perception of yourself is raised to another level. You come to feel the world and other people as another self. You feel that other people, along with all organisms existing in the universe, are connected and one with you. When you look at the world with such awareness, a great love and compassion for the world and its people come pouring out of you. And you start actualizing in reality the world of the consciousness you felt. It's all about connecting with the world and connecting with people. Your consciousness extends to you, not to you alone but to you, connected to the whole.

If you've realized that you're one with the cosmos but can't feel that you're one with other people, that is not yet full enlightenment. That means you're still making judgments and discriminations about people with your awareness on the level of thought and emotion. Of course, it's true that each of us have different thoughts and emotions. That's why, basically, we must respect our differences. If we are at the level of thought and emotion, though, we can't help but perceive ourselves as different from each other. We have to go to a deeper level of consciousness. Everyone is finally interconnected when we reach into our inner consciousness and keep going, feeling our true nature that exists at the very bottom of our heart.

In the depths of their hearts, all people have the same true nature as you, the same true heart. Your true heart is no different from that of others. Why? We've all come from the same Source, from the true nature of the cosmos.

Feel and believe that all people share this. Meet, talk, and connect with people, holding that unchanging faith in your heart. Then you'll be able to approach everyone comfortably and naturally with an open heart and mind.

Your ultimate identity is the self in which everything is interconnected as one. I express this in a single sentence:

"I am one soul in one community in one spirit."

"One spirit" means the one world of the cosmos, a great, bright world of consciousness and energy. It's the invisible, spiritual world. "One community" is the confines within which we live, as big as the universe and as small as the Earth. It refers to the visible, material world. "One soul" means the individual particle that is your self. "I am one soul in one community in one spirit"—this means that I am one particle living in the community of the Earth, of the cosmos, connected with the great spirit of the universe. This is the essence of who I am, seen through enlightened consciousness. I'm not a separate individual, far away from everything else, but a being connected organically with all things, within the one community and spirit of the cosmos. "I am one soul in one community in one spirit." What enables you to realize this and feel it with your whole body, your whole consciousness, is Pineal Gland Meditation.

What's most important, though, is what happens after the meditation is done. The things you perceived as one during meditation with your eyes closed may again appear as separate. The properties of the material world, which we perceive through the senses as separate, start encroaching on your awareness as soon as you open your eyes. What should you do when that happens?

Your physical eyes see a world of separation. However, you should now be able to see the world with your spiritual eye, transcending your physical vision. You see with integrated consciousness, which your pineal gland has awakened.

Why don't you practice this right now? Stare at something in front of you. It doesn't matter what it is—an object, a person, nature. Just stare at it as you would normally look at anything with your physical eyes.

Now look again, but add another eye. Being aware of the pineal gland in your brain, look at the same object with the eye of your pineal gland, your third eye. In this state, try to be aware of your brain, your body, your whole self. And try to sense how that feeling is different from what you felt before, when you looked only with your physical eyes.

Some people will feel a big difference, others a subtle one. Generally when you see only with your physical eyes you just look, without thinking anything in particular. You're using only your visual sense. When you're looking with the eye of your pineal gland, though, don't you have the feeling that it's not just your eyes looking, but *you* seeing? Don't you sense that you're looking at the object while connected with yourself, with your consciousness focusing inward? You feel that all areas of your brain are operating, not just your vision. If you keep focusing and are sensitive enough, you may feel a clear, bright energy coming down from the crown of your head and sinking into your spine. It is turning on the light of consciousness in your brain.

Looking with the eye of the pineal gland is seeing the world while you are connected with yourself. You're not looking through glasses colored by worldly ideas or your own emotions, but you are instead seeing the world solely through the consciousness of the true self. "I" am looking, not someone or something else. This self is you, the state of Divine Brain, which the sense of peace and equilibrium has awakened in the brain. It is opening the eye of the divinity within you, the eye of the Creator. The pineal gland is a connector, interconnecting everything, the eye of the One seeing through illusion to perceive the truth.

Now open the eye of your pineal gland, become a Divine Brain, and look at the world. See, interpret, and gain insight into the world with your spiritual eye, with an awareness of connection, unity, and peace. You'll see fundamental solutions that can change reality.

Pineal Gland Meditation gives inner strength that enables us to alter reality. One of the reasons we are troubled is the gap between our ideals and reality. Our ideals—what we want—are lofty and big, but the reality we face is so small, so trivial, that we suffer from the gulf between the two. The world we see through meditation is truly whole and complete, a place where all are connected and one. It's the utopia that you and I and humanity dream of, a place of love, peace, blessings, oneness, fulfillment, and bright light. It's the unseen world of consciousness, the World of Heaven. But what about the reality we see when we open our eyes? Separation, competition, envy, jealousy, hatred, violence, discrimination, things we do not want—these run rampant. This is the World of Earth, distinct from the World of Heaven.

Our task is to move the World of Heaven, the utopia we see through meditation, into the World of Earth, the reality in which we live. Pineal Gland Meditation gives us the power to download and move the information and images of the higher consciousness we've seen through meditation into the real world. Our lives are composed of an endless series of images gained through experience, and those individual images come together to form the reality and future of the human race. Humanity's future is a joint project, a huge mosaic we're all creating together.

One thing is certain: we can picture only as much as we've seen. It's difficult to make into reality what we can't bring to mind in the world of our consciousness. All creation begins with ideas, within the world of consciousness. That's why each of us need to raise our consciousness, making it higher and brighter. The higher and brighter our consciousness, the more we can download bright, positive images that will contribute to ourselves, other people, and the world. When consciousness is low and dark, not only does it not help you or other people, but in severe cases it can attract dark, negative, harmful information. Each of our lives is realized precisely according to the brightness of our consciousness, which is the level of our energy.

If we continue living only for the visible world, the material World of Earth, we will have no hope. We will endlessly relive our experiences of frustration, anxiety, and anger. We should strive to lift our eyes and look upward, connecting with the world of bright, higher consciousness. It is our duty to manifest in visible reality the unseen world of higher consciousness, the World of Heaven—to make the world on earth as it is in heaven.

After awakening on Mt. Moak to the essence of who I am, I thought deeply about what I would do in the future. During my meditative practice at this time, two future visions for humanity unfolded before me, one after another. One was a peaceful world of people living together in harmony with nature, a world overflowing with joy, happiness, and vitality. The other was full of myriad tragedies, humanity suffering amid natural disasters, rampant disease, and endless selfishness and greed.

The stark contrast between the beauty and the wretchedness of these two worlds tore deep into my heart, and I realized what I needed to do. I resolved to dedicate myself to realizing the world of peace and harmony. I felt that my task was to help people recover their true selves, to make a happier, more peaceful world. This became the vision I wanted to achieve over the rest of my life.

Decades later, I now have two attitudes when I look at the world. One is worry and concern; the other, hope. Which of the two worlds do you think humanity is headed toward? Just seeing the things that are happening as a result of ever-increasing environmental pollution and global warming does, in fact, bring anxious foreboding. As scientists studying the global environment have been warning us, we'll reach a point of no return if we continue on our present course.

What is the true solution to the problems humanity faces? How are we supposed to find that solution, and where? You can now probably guess what that solution is, to some degree. The true solution is found in the invisible world of consciousness. The awareness of each individual must grow brighter and rise higher. If most people are disconnected from their true selves, from other people, and nature and if they fail to perceive the world where all are interconnected and one, then this consciousness of separation, disconnection, and competition will inevitably cause still more serious problems. We will only be able to diagnose and discover solutions to the problems we face when people's consciousness rises higher and grows brighter than the consciousness that caused the problems and they're able to gain an insightful, wide viewpoint of the present material world without being attached only to that visible world.

What we need now to resolve the problems of our world is tolerance and empathy. We cannot help but tolerate each other once we realize that we are truly one. If we, especially religions, races, and nations, still divide and categorize each other, reject rather than embrace one another, we haven't yet deeply realized or have turned our backs on the truth that we are one.

Tolerance and empathy stem from an open consciousness that considers the position of the opposite side, not only its own. If we understand both sides, we'll find it easier to reach a point of harmony, one where we help each other without anyone getting hurt. This is a win-win approach. If more people come to have this consciousness, a consensus will form that allows us to solve our personal conflicts and, on a larger scale, to solve conflicts between nations and religions.

The problems of global environmental pollution and global warming are developing because the connection between humanity and nature has been broken. If we realize that we and nature are one connected organism, we feel an urge to take care of nature as we take care of ourselves. Could it be that the attitudes we have in failing to care for ourselves are the same ones we have in dealing with other people and even nature? If you love yourself, you can't help but love other people and nature, too. Ultimately, a fundamental solution for all the problems begins in recovering your connection with yourself.

As I look on the world in these times, I'm not letting go of hope. I consider this to be the Era of Shinmyung. When you attain Shinmyung, you are able to access the information of the unseen world through illuminated consciousness. Uploading and downloading the information our brains need, we more actively exchange information.

Surprisingly, the Era of Shinmyung is already being manifested in the material world of the present, thanks to information technology such as television, computers, the internet, smartphones, and social media. Just press a button and the unseen world spreads out before you on a screen. Through technology, we can watch things happening in distant countries, physically beyond our vision. We can video chat with friends around the world, and we can share our feelings and information in real time through texts, images, video, and so on. The scope of information coming into our brains is no longer limited to experiences and knowledge unique to us. Opening our brains wide, we now listen to others, accessing their knowledge and experience and sharing useful information. As our brains connect, the range of our information and our consensus is widening in an unlimited way. The online world could almost be considered a collective brain of humanity. Viewed from the perspective of material civilization, the Era of Shinmyung is becoming a reality.

If more positive and inspiring information continues to spread, humanity could be connected by a consciousness of love, tolerance, unity, and peace. We will be able to move our ideal world into reality and usher in an era of spiritual civilization. For that to happen, we must each believe that this ideal world can be realized and not end as nothing but a dream. We should make use of the fact that we now live in a world with incredibly powerful information technology, unprecedented in human history—a world in which people all around the globe can instantly check the same information on their TVs and smartphones.

Now during this Era of Shinmyung, energy waves of a high frequency are coming down to us, energy that awakens the pineal gland. Don't limit yourself to any frame any longer. Let yourself be truly open, connecting with heaven. And connect with the world and its people. None of us has a small, insignificant life. We are all incarnations of the Creator, having consciousness with infinite potential, bright like the sun and vast like the universe.

People who want to connect with heaven are "people of heaven." They are not determined by birth, social structure, or any belief system. Anyone can be a person of heaven if they live with a consciousness connected with heaven—cosmic energy and consciousness. The brightness shining within each of us makes that possible for us, too. You can feel heaven inside you and realize heaven on earth, here and now. You don't need to wait until you die to go to heaven. You can create heaven around you and within you while you are living now.

This is how I describe the state in which the divinity in the brain has awakened, transforming its home into a Divine Brain.

"The one spirit has come down and dwells in my brain,
and numinous energy of heaven flows in my body and limbs."

The one spirit, heaven, already dwells in you. Focus on your pineal gland. Try to feel the one spirit, divinity, that has descended into your brain. And feel the numinous energy of heaven, the energy of life, flowing in your body and limbs. Being aware in this moment with your brain that your heart is beating, your lungs breathing—that is the great love and blessing of heaven. **That is a miracle.**

Feel the infinite life energy of heaven continuously supporting you, never leaving you even for a moment. Bright light, great love, and eternal life energy are working in you right now. You have come into this life with that energy and you will leave it with that energy.

Gently close your eyes and say this to yourself:

I am bright light.

I am great love.

I am eternal life.

I am light, love, and eternal life.

Receive this message and accept it. Simply download heaven's energy of love and blessings. This is a spring that never dries, the energy of infinite joy. The energy of happiness will fill all the cells in your body, and every moment of your life will be a joy. No conditions must be met to receive this. It's enough to just accept that energy, as you accept the life you've been given and the sunlight shining on you. Accept the unconditional, eternal love and blessings of heaven. And use and share the energy of love and joy inside you.

Connect

Download

Share

Doing these three things is enough. Never forget that everything begins with you, or more precisely, through the connection with the divinity inside you. Don't worry any longer, for you can always activate your pineal gland, your connector, to download the power and energy you want.

You can attract cosmic energy of infinite joy, gratitude, love, and blessings, or you can attract the energy of sadness, despair, anxiety, and resentment. What energy will you connect with and download? It depends on you.

Why not make a habit of connecting with your self every morning before you start your day? Right after you've gotten up in the morning, or after you've taken a shower or had your morning tea or gone for a morning walk, just sit, close your eyes, and focus within. Feel the power of your core, feel the soul in your heart, and connect with divinity through the channel of your pineal gland.

And declare this three times loudly as you raise your arms:

"I am the master of my brain! I am the master of my life!"

Try it now. Affirm to yourself that you are the true master of your brain and life. Even when you are in a moment of hardship and pain, you can choose this, and you can choose it right now. Why are you worried? No conditions are required. Just choose it. Knowing this, the power of consciousness, is enlightenment, and it is what I really wish to convey to you.

You are no longer alone. You're not a lonely, isolated being, for the breath of heaven is with you, inside you, in each and every moment. It is the life energy always shining in you, never missing a moment.

Flowers of true love and creation bloom there. When the flowers that each of us blooms all harmonize together, when the heaven in you connects with the heaven in others, we will tremble together in oneness.

Now open the eye of your pineal gland and see.
Everything will be connected.
And everything will be perfect as it is.
All you have to do is CONNECT.

Toward a World of Connection and Oneness

On the journey to connecting with your true self through Pineal Gland Meditation, there are two things you have inevitably met: humanity and the Earth.

As members of their communities and as mature global citizens, many people feel concern for the future of humanity and the Earth. They make great efforts to leave a better world for future generations. However, the humanity and Earth that you have met through Pineal Gland Meditation will appear quite different from what you knew before. Just as your conception of "self" has grown, your understanding of humanity and the Earth has expanded to include dimensions that were once beyond your reach.

Through Pineal Gland Meditation, you feel that you are a single body, a unit of oneness connected with nature, with all life, and with the universe. When such connection arises, the way you feel about humanity and the Earth is much more than the ideas of citizenship or moral obligation that you've been taught. Your humanity becomes an extension of your own self, another manifestation of who you are. People who have experienced this connectivity, not just intellectually but with their whole bodies, develop a deep sense of caring and affection for all living things and for the world itself. Not only that, they also feel a strong sense of responsibility and solidarity, a yearning for everyone's well-being and for the elevation of human consciousness. That's what happened to me about 40 years ago on Mt. Moak, when I met with cosmic energy and cosmic mind, my true essence. Many people who practice Pineal Gland Meditation—people of all ages and backgrounds—have experienced this same feeling.

The way to assure not only individual health and happiness but also sustainability and peace for the Earth starts with each of us recovering our connection with our true nature and essence—which is pure energy and life—and with our divinity. That pure consciousness and energy are the key that enables us to connect with everything and become who we truly are.

Have you heard about the Go competition between Lee Sedol and AI AlphaGo that took place in South Korea in the spring of 2016? Lee Sedol is a grandmaster Go player, and AlphaGo is a computer program made by Google. In this competition, Lee Sedol lost to AlphaGo 1-4. Many people were shocked, and I was no exception. I thought that no matter how competent a computer might be, it could never exceed the intuition, judgment, creativity, mental flexibility, and responsive speed exhibited by the best Go players. With the development of AI, though, it has become difficult to say that intellectual abilities such as studying, thinking, and decision-making are unique human characteristics. If high cognitive ability is no longer a special attribute of humans, then what is the true value of humans?

Artificial intelligence is becoming increasingly common in our daily lives. Robots order products for us and clean for us and keep our homes secure. They write news articles, translate, and converse with us via chatbots. They drive cars. It is said that in the future, AI will be capable of performing work that demands a high level of intelligence, such as diagnosing illness and conducting surgery, or performing accounting, investment, or legal consulting.

Humankind has entered a new Industrial Revolution, experts say. The world has already seen three other Industrial Revolutions: the first one began with the invention of steam engines; the second was brought about by electricity and mass production; and the third is represented by computers and automation. Now we enter the fourth Industrial Revolution, which has fused human intelligence with machine intelligence. Scientists predict that we will be living in a whole new world, one that is entirely different from what we've known before.

What kind of future society will the advancement of technology bring? Some say that the development of innovative products and enhanced productivity will fill our lives with boundless material comfort. On the other hand, there is a great deal of worry that people will lose their jobs to robots, and that extreme wealth will be amassed by a small minority of people—such as the owners and CEOs of massive IT corporations—and society will become increasingly polarized.

What do you think? What kind of world do you think we'll be living in? Or rather, what kind of world do you want to live in? And what kind of role do you feel you can play in creating that world?

I've decided to raise my hand in favor of hope. If artificial intelligence becomes an object of fear, that would not be because of AI but because of the consciousness of humans using it for harmful aims. If human consciousness is the cause of the problem, the solution also becomes clear. Human consciousness must expand to a level where people think beyond their individual selves or the group to which they belong but instead take all of humankind into consideration. That's when technology can be used for the health and happiness of all of humankind to create a true, whole new world.

I dream that our spiritual awakening and insight will be used beyond our personal lives, expanding to every domain of society, including politics, economics, culture, education, and the arts. I imagine that the systems we have created will be re-evaluated and newly organized under the greater shared goal of actualizing real human value and peace for the Earth. For example, if AI could handle most of the activity of production that humans have performed, that could free us to engage in more creative and humanitarian activities. Working just four hours a day and taking the rest of our time for our personal lives may be a fantasy we can only dream about right now, but in the future it could become a common lifestyle.

The considerable resources now used to maintain and manage societal systems—collecting taxes, executing legislation, mediating conflict, maintaining public order, and electing representatives—could instead be used for the welfare of the population. Wouldn't it be possible to create a society that guarantees enough income for every human to maintain at least a decent standard of living, regardless of where people are born or whose children they are or what job they have? Shouldn't everyone live without having to worry about where they'll sleep or where the next meal is coming from?

A great deal of change could come to education, as well. Rather than education that conveys knowledge and skills, it could become education that helps everyone discover and actualize their latent potential and passion. Instead of tests that differentiate superiority and inferiority through competition, there would be collaboration where each person expresses and shares their creativity and passion to their heart's content. Education would be re-oriented from producing functional humans to producing humans who possess upright character and integrity.

If we advance through the fourth Industrial Revolution with an awakened and expanded consciousness, we will be met with a fifth Industrial Revolution that demonstrates a quality different from those we have seen thus far. The values of separation, competition, and material success are the paradigms that have led the change from the first to the fourth Industrial Revolutions. These values brought with them the dramatically swift development of material civilization, represented by convenience and efficiency, but they also put humankind face to face with the dire problems of unsustainable growth and environmental crisis.

I believe that the fifth Industrial Revolution will take place not through a revolution of technology, but through a paradigm shift in perception of value. Rather than separation, competition, and success, the new values of integration, cooperation, and completion will direct our choices and actions. Through this kind of shift, the true potential of the technical advancement produced by the fourth Industrial Revolution can be manifested. Without such a change, people will be confined within the framework of their preconceptions in a situation akin to tending only to their own garden despite having enough power to cultivate the Earth.

In a value system based on competition, the winner gets the monopoly, along with feelings of superiority. For values formed through cooperation, however, everything belongs to everyone, so there's no need for any one person to feel a sense of superiority or inferiority. When this happens, jobs will not be ascribed higher or lower status. Rather than aiming for higher prestige or status in society, the purpose of life will be for each person to contribute to society by becoming the best they can be.

Humanity still has groups of political, religious, and economic elite who use violence and force to hold onto their vested interests. Conflict and war are as ubiquitous as ever. However, if human beings' state of spiritual awakening grows and human consciousness becomes free of ego and prejudice and knows its ultimate value, it will become impossible to use distorted information to restrict or control the minds and lives of people. And instead of seeing differences in nationality or race, people will come to see the divinity within all human beings and in all existence. When that time comes, countries and national borders will no longer have meaning, and a true Earth village can be realized.

At present, we focus on researching and using content produced by consciousness, such as ideas, emotions, and imagination, but it won't be long before consciousness itself is studied and applied to life. Though it's already possible to know the true nature of consciousness through meditation, it will be proven scientifically as well. Consciousness is where matter and spirit, science and religion come together. Through new discoveries and understanding about consciousness, science and religion will be integrated, and matter and spirit will be integrated. The era in which systematized religion controls human spirituality will pass, and there will come the true normalization of enlightenment. All people will discover and actualize the spirituality within themselves, and enlightenment will become common sense, a regular part of everyday life.

When this kind of change arises in human consciousness, the greatest project in the era of the fifth Industrial Revolution will be the recovery of the Earth's environment. A sustainable Earth—the restoration of the Earth's healthy and beautiful environment as the base that supports the continued evolution and growth of humanity—would surely be a project to which all of humankind would contribute knowledge, skills, wisdom, and love. Through that project, as we love each other and overflow with creative energy, humanity will recover its true nature, rising bravely toward the great goal of completion.

The key to succeeding in this great project is the development of the empathic ability of our brain. This comes from pure energy and consciousness connecting all things as one. It is because we have empathy that we can go beyond separation, to commune and feel the pain of others and comfort them.

If we humans did not have empathic ability, what would be the reason for us to continue existing on the Earth? We know that humans are the biggest cause of the problems the Earth currently faces. Looking at it from the Earth's perspective, the humans who are destroying the Earth's ecosystems are likely the biggest pain in the neck. If you told AI—which makes determinations based on data, without any emotions or bias—to find the fastest and most effective way to recover the Earth's ecosystems, it would probably suggest the improvement of humans. It might even recommend the elimination of humans.

In spite of that, humans are the only thing we can stake our hope on. Would a whale in the Pacific Ocean be concerned for a rhino on the plains of the savanna just because they're in the same situation of being endangered? Of course, animals protect their young and can help other creatures. But humans are the beings that can expand empathy to encompass all life, and therefore we are the beings who can look after the entire Earth. Humans have caused many problems on the Earth, but it is also humans who have the power and the hope to solve those problems.

The key to solving problems such as violence, discrimination, inequality, human rights violations, and environmental destruction is to be found not in systems or technology but in recovering empathy. Breaking free from the ego and helping others unconditionally is the power of a consciousness that can perceive and embrace all life forms as one. What connects one person's heart with another's isn't smartphones or the internet or social media. When empathetic ability comes alive and heart-to-heart connections are made, we can avoid a cold and miserable future in which people have close connections on the physical level—through social systems and information technology—but are disconnected spiritually and filled with a sense of hollow futility.

People must have a shared sentiment about these values and work together in order to make these changes. It wouldn't mean much if only one person had a smartphone. It's because many people have them that connections are made and great power is demonstrated. Likewise, the majority of people must awaken their consciousness and become connected to create the solutions to the problems we face.

It's difficult for anyone to present the perfect answer to the various problems faced by humanity and the Earth. It's clear, however, that it isn't the leaders, experts, government, or corporations that hold the key to solving them. The answer is found in every one of us.

As of yet, the new world that I described earlier is just imagination and potentiality. You might think this dream is impossible because it is too grand. Because our brains have mainly been socialized for competition, it may feel strange to suddenly call upon the sense of peace and cooperation in your brain. But when you're connected through Pineal Gland Meditation with the world of infinite energy and consciousness within your brains, you feel it. We feel how much we want to be connected, how great a sense of hope and freedom is offered by opening ourselves up and connecting with a world bigger than ourselves, and we feel how great a sense of love, creative power, and deep peace there is inside us. If our brains can feel that and that discovery makes our hearts soar, and if we sincerely want and choose it, we will be able to create that world as our reality.

I believe that when we are truly connected with ourselves,

our dreams will finally come together as one. If, through this book, your dream and mine have become connected, I am grateful. I hope with all my heart that all the choices we make and the steps we take can be connected to achieve humankind's greatest potential and most beautiful dream together on this Earth.

P. S.

I'd like ask you to share with others any inspiration and awakening you've received through this book. One of the simplest ways you can do that is leaving an online review. Write down your thoughts about the book on your favorite bookselling or review site so that others can be inspired to learn more. Thank you from the bottom of my heart.

Acknowledgments

I would like to express my sincere thanks to the editorial team that continues to bring my books to life. From the Korean manuscript editing by Hyerin Moon, Jiyoung Oh, and Steve Kim to the translation by Daniel Graham and Michelle Seo to the English editing by Nicole Dean, Phyllis Elving, and Michela Mangiaracina, each person beautifully shined and polished the words I am honored to bring to the world. I am especially grateful to Hyerin Moon at Best Life Media, who managed the entire editing process.

The visuals were no less impressive, with the cover and interior design by Kiryl Lysenka and the illustrations by Eunjung Shin that brought the concepts to life.

I would also like to thank the many people who shared their stories of transformation with Pineal Gland Meditation, and all of the people around the world who are using Pineal Gland Meditation to connect to their true selves and divinity.

About the Author

Ilchi Lee is a visionary, educator, mentor, and innovator who has dedicated his life to teaching energy principles and developing methods to nurture the full potential of the brain.

For almost four decades, his life's mission has been to help people harness their own creative power. For this goal, he has developed many successful mind-body training methods, including Body & Brain Yoga and Brain Education. His principles and methods have inspired many people around the world to live healthier and happier lives.

Lee is a *New York Times* bestselling author who has penned more than 40 books, including *The Call of Sedona: Journey of the Heart, The Power Brain: Five Steps to Upgrading Your Brain Operating System*, and *I've Decided to Live 120 Years: The Ancient Secret to Longevity, Vitality, and Life Transformation.*

He is also a well-respected humanitarian who has been working with the United Nations and other organizations for global peace. He began the Earth Citizen Movement, a global drive to raise awareness of the values of earth citizenship and put them into practice.

Lee serves as president of the University of Brain Education, the Global Cyber University, and the International Brain Education Association. For more information about Ilchi Lee and his work, visit ilchi.com.

Resources

Body & Brain Yoga Tai Chi Classes

The 100 Body & Brain Yoga and Tai Chi centers in the United States are one of the best ways you can make the meditations, exercises, and principles introduced in this book a meaningful part of your daily life.

BODY&BRAIN

They offer classes, workshops, and individual sessions based on Ilchi Lee's Brain Education principles and methods. The expert instructors and center community also provide advice and support for your continued growth and life creation.

Special Offer for the Readers of This Book

Bring a copy of this book to a Body & Brain Yoga and Tai Chi center anywhere in the United States and get 50% off an Introductory Session. During this 45-minute private session, an instructor will check your flexibility, balance, breathing, energy, and stress levels and recommend a customized practice plan tailored to your physical, mental, emotional, and/or spiritual needs. This special offer ends June 30, 2020. Find a center near you at BodynBrain.com.

Brain Recharge App

Brain Recharge is a web service and app with 100+ brain-based guided meditations curated for total mind-

body wellness. Brain Recharge meditations activate your brain power and natural healing ability with light, sound, and vibration. Its content is backed by 40 years of research from meditation expert and creator of Brain Education, Ilchi Lee. To learn more, visit BrainRecharge.com or download the app at your favorite app store.

Brain Education TV

Brain Education TV is a lifestyle and consciousness movement YouTube channel created by Ilchi Lee. It features videos of brain tips, inspiring stories, meditations, and exercises that help you take back your

brain to create the life you want. Learn more at YouTube.com/ BrainEducationTV.

ConnectByIlchi.com

The book's official website. Visit to learn more about Pineal Gland Meditation and other exercises in *Connect: How to Find Clarity and Expand Your Consciousness with Pineal Gland Meditation.* Find all of the meditation tools introduced in the book to enhance your practice. Other book formats are also available.

Books of Related Interest

The following books have useful information to deepen your Pineal Gland Meditation practice. See them all and more of Ilchi Lee's books at BestLifeMedia.com.

I've Decided to Live 120 Years

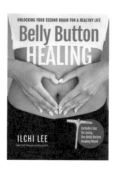

Belly Button Healing

Living Tao

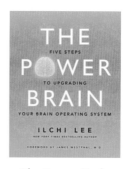

The Power Brain

LifeParticle Meditation

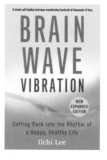

Brain Wave Vibration

Cut this image to use as a temporary LifeParticle Card.

Cut this image to use as a temporary LifeParticle card.